The Westchester Review™

A LITERARY JOURNAL OF WRITERS FROM THE HUDSON TO THE SOUND

This year we initiated a contest
for writers under 30 in the categories
of prose and poetry. We were delighted
with the enthusiastic response and
are pleased to present the winners
in this, our sixth issue.

Allison Rosenthal, Prose — *Unsound*
Sarah Levine, Poetry — *Bang-Bang*

THE WESTCHESTER REVIEW

FOUNDER AND PUBLISHER
JoAnn Duncan Terdiman

MANAGING EDITOR
Naomi L. Lipman

EDITORS
Stephanie Kaplan Cohen
Judith Naomi Fish
Lesleigh Forsyth
Joan Motyka
Amy Ralston Seife

CONSULTANTS
Amy Bauman
Mary Borowka
Steve Borowka
Matt Colonell
Susan Duncan
Gilbert Forsyth
Bob Glass
George Gottlieb
Ruth Obernbreit
Rick Wingate

ART DIRECTOR
Orlando Adiao

EDITOR IN CHIEF EMERITA
Louise Albert

The Westchester Review is published annually. The editors welcome previously unpublished prose and poetry by established and emerging writers living, working, or studying in New York State's Westchester County.

We read manuscripts year-round. Electronic submissions, with cover letter, may be sent to submissions@westchesterreview.com. Complete submissions guidelines are available online at www.westchesterreview.com.

Manuscripts may be mailed to
The Westchester Review
P.O. Box 246H
Scarsdale, NY 10583

The Westchester Review is a sponsored project of Fractured Atlas, a non-profit arts service organization. Contributions for the purposes of The Westchester Review must be made payable to Fractured Atlas and are tax-deductible to the extent permitted by law.

Library of Congress Control Number: 2012951578

ISBN: 978-0-615-71550-6

CONTENTS

DRAMA

POETRY

Unsound

Allison Rosenthal

I'M ONLY WRITING THIS BECAUSE MY SISTER SAID I HAVE TO. SHE SAID if I don't, they'll put me somewhere I don't want to be, and I said where? and she said somewhere bright and sterile and where there are a lot of people and not so many animals, and I said how do I know you're not lying? and she said because she's my sister, and she's sick of doing my IRS forms for me and paying my insurance and driving me places and something else I can't remember and explaining me to people and this is my last chance or she's giving me up to the state. I said *no comprendo* because my dad used to say that's what you say to people when they're talking to you and you just want them to go away. She said that's not helping my case any and then she left.

But before she left, she told me that she'd show this notebook to a doctor and he'd tell her whether I should go to the place I don't want to be, and if I didn't want to go there I'd better do a good job of proving I'm not crazy. I said what should I write in the notebook? and she said anything you want, as long as it's about yourself and it's not crazy. I said I'm not crazy, it's everyone else that's crazy, not me, and that's when she got fed up and left.

So I'm writing in this notebook to show I'm not crazy, because I'm happy with my life here and I don't want to go to any place my sister says I don't want to go to. So, doctor, I'm not crazy. You're crazy. You're crazy and everyone else around me is crazy and my sister is crazy and the kids at the school I work at are crazy and President Obama is crazy

1

and I'm trying to think of other people I've heard of but I can't remember any. The people who write National Geographic are crazy because the magazine is all about people and not enough about birds. I like it when they have pictures of birds. I've gotten National Geographic for eighteen years, and I've cut out every picture they've had of birds in the magazine since I've gotten it and I've taped them on my window. The birds look very pretty with the light from the sun shining through them.

I CALLED MY SISTER and asked her what I should write about, and she said why don't you write about what you did today. So what I did today was I went to work, which is being a janitor at a middle school. I like it because most of the time I don't have to talk to anyone. There's another janitor besides me, but I clean my half of the building and he cleans his half of the building and sometimes in the morning he tells me good morning but when I grunt or say *no comprendo* he goes away. The teachers don't bother to talk to me, and the kids won't look at me because one of my eyes goes the other way from the other one. So I go around with my cart full of cleaning fluid, and I wipe cleaning fluid all over the doorknobs and I mop it up when one of the kids throws up. I like it. When there are classes the hallways are quiet and I can whistle and no one minds. I'm a very good whistler, doctor. I don't do it crappy like most people. I do it like I'm an actual bird and I'm looking for a mate, or something. I don't really want a mate though.

I like other animals besides birds. I have a rat. I didn't name him. He named himself, but he won't tell me what his name is. I brought him to work once, and he was very good and stayed in my pocket most of the time, but one of the teachers saw him sticking his little head out and I had to talk to the principal and she told me rats were dirty and they carried plagues. I said this rat was very clean because I had just seen him licking himself this morning, but she said not to bring him to school again ever or I'd lose my job, and I don't want to lose my job.

I like reading about animals in National Geographic. I like the birds, like I said earlier, but I also like reading the articles, even if they're about people. I like reading words like antiquarian. I don't care what it means, but I like rolling the word in my mouth. Antiquarian. It sounds like it means something blue.

I JUST MADE MYSELF an egg-and-ketchup sandwich. I cooked the egg myself and I ate it while I was doing my Rubik's Cube. I can do a Rubik's Cube pretty fast, you know.

I bought the eggs at the supermarket yesterday. I saw my favorite cashier, the one who stands under the number seven. His nametag says Joe and he has this mustache that goes out from his face, and when he smiles you can't see his mouth but you can see the mustache move up and down like Jell-O. He smiles at me sometimes. I like it better when he doesn't.

I talk to Joe more than I talk to other people. He says hi, how are you, and I say okay, and he says paper or plastic, and I say plastic because I like ripping the little plastic tabs off the bag, and I give him my twenty dollar bill and he says thank you, and then he gives me change and says have a nice day and I leave. He didn't smile at me yesterday. He didn't really look at me, either, he just looked at a picture of a girl in a tabloid in the aisle across from him. I didn't mind.

I should probably tell you about my friend, not Joe but my actual friend named Kei who's from Japan and doesn't talk. He doesn't actually know he's my friend but that's okay. He goes to the middle school I work at, and he doesn't speak English very well. He mostly follows around Mr. Tomoki who's the only teacher who speaks Japanese. He started last week. The other kids don't talk to him, but I think he must be okay with that because he doesn't talk to them either. He doesn't talk to me. He doesn't call me "hey mister could you please mop up Jimmy's Gatorade that I spilled" like the other kids do. That's why I like him.

Do you think I should let Kei know he's my friend, doctor? I'm not sure he'd understand me if I tried.

My mother called today to see how I am. I'm good like always. She reminded me to vacuum this weekend and to call my sister to wish her a happy birthday. I did, yesterday, even though it's not her birthday till tomorrow, but I figured I'd forget if I didn't already do it.

TODAY I WATCHED KEI'S GYM CLASS through the window in the door. When people passed by, I pretended I was cleaning the doorknobs, which is one of the most important parts of my job, because of E. coli I think. No one asked me what I was doing, though. The kids were playing volleyball. Kei wasn't very good as far as I could tell, but that's okay because no one really noticed him. This one blond girl hit it so high, though, she almost hit the ceiling and knocked down the ropes they use for the Presidential Fitness Test.

When the class let out, Kei walked by me, and I looked at him and he looked at me and he didn't smile, which I was okay with. The smilers are the bad ones, the ones who are nice at the beginning but then they go and throw up red Jell-O and I'm the one who cleans it up. I saw Kei again later, after lunch. I don't know where he was coming from but Mr. Tomoki wasn't with him this time. I went up to him and asked him if he knew where his next class was. He said "Yes," which was good because I was afraid he was going to say no and I wouldn't be able to help him because I didn't know where his next class was. He didn't notice how one of my eyes goes the other way from the other, I could tell because he was looking at his shoes.

My shoes are hiking boots because that's what my sister said I should get, so I did. They were hard and uncomfortable until I took them off and dropped a brick on each of them, which softened them up a little, because they were squished. Now they're fine and I wear them every day.

I HAD A DREAM LAST NIGHT where I was playing laser tag, only it wasn't real lasers, it was Silly String that stuck on your clothes so everyone knew you had been hit when you had been hit, and the person who was hit the most had to stand on a table while everyone laughed at him. I never had to be that person, but I was scared that I would, so I threw away my Silly String and hoped that maybe everyone else would too, after they saw me do it. No one did, though. So I spent the whole time hiding behind a trash can, and when I woke up I realized I hadn't gotten any Silly String on my clothes, but I also hadn't played laser tag at all, so what was even the point, really.

KEI AND I TALKED TODAY. Here's what we said: Kei said do you know where the water fountain is please and I said over there and he said okay thank you and then he said do you talk to other teachers? and I said I'm not a teacher anyway so why would I and he said I don't know, who do you talk to then? and I said I have a rat and I don't think he knew what a rat was, because he said oh, okay and then he went over to the water fountain.

I felt sad after, though, sadder than I had been after my Silly String dream.

I DIDN'T see Kei today.

TODAY either.

MY SISTER CALLED TODAY. She said she was in the area and did I need her to bring my laundry to the laundromat? I said what for, it's going to get dirty again anyway and she said see, this is why I don't offer you things like this, and then I remembered about you, doctor, and how I'm not crazy and I said yes, thank you, you can bring my laundry to the laundromat, and she said are you kidding me? and I said no, I'm not kidding you, you can bring my laundry to the laundromat. So she did, and now I'm wearing clean pajamas and I don't feel any different.

I HAVEN'T seen Kei all week.

I ASKED A TEACHER where Kei was and he said didn't you notice? Kei went back to Japan and I said no, I didn't notice, but thanks anyway but I was actually thinking *no comprendo,* and I looked down at my hiking boots and he looked down at his brown shoes and he walked away and I didn't and the sun was shining through the cafeteria window, it was shining because it was making the world hot outside and Japan was the land of the rising sun, or shining sun or something, I read in National Geographic, and I'm tying and untying my shoelaces over and over again because I can never tie them tight enough, and if they're not tight enough my feet will fall out and I won't have anything to stand on and

I'll fall off and it'll be like I'm the one covered in Silly String and I'm on the table and everyone's laughing and throwing things and no one wants to talk to me because I don't know how to talk to anyone and my rat's gone missing and my clean clothes are exactly the same as my dirty ones, unless someone's spilled Gatorade on them and I have to clean it up and I have to clean everything up

MY SISTER TOOK ME TO HERE, this place where I don't want to be. I got this book back after she gave it to you, doctor, so you must think I'm crazy just like she does, but I'm not crazy, you're crazy, I'm the only normal one because what if you're just pictures in a magazine and it's the birds reading about us? You don't know, you might just think you know, so I'm not talking to anyone again because what's even the point, I'm still here even though I try to *comprendo*, but the truth is I just can't and neither can Kei and neither can you or my sister and we're all trying for the same thing but some are just better at it than others. ◇

Bang-Bang

Sarah Levine

I went messy for Begonia.
Her gooseneck and hobnobbing.
How well she wears her white shoes and white socks.

She makes my tongue dumb
And when I lick her knees
I taste the heads of hammers.

I saw her first in mother's car
When she stepped through the street
In only the arms of a sweater.

My heart shot
Bang-Bang.
I couldn't stop licking the window clean.

I saw her second by the schoolhouse
Speaking to no one but the sky—
Air punches like bullets from a broken gun.

And I wanted to jump off my school desk and wrestle a thrush into
    her throat.

I saw her third at mother's funeral
When she put her hand inside my pocket
Smiled with teeth bigger than light bulbs.

And I felt clean as if someone just threw me up into the world.

I am no longer a boy put together the wrong way.
I have a girl—
I have the girl who meets me under the trees.

And she lets me look close enough to see the hair on her chin.

When I look I get hungry
Like a wolf for his rabbit.
My heart grows loud and messy.

And I realize I know nothing.

So I sock stalks of corn in the face until the sun has had enough.

I roll in puddles and plead for summer lightning to lift me off my feet
For I love you.

My hands and teeth and bloody pulp of a heart
Love you.
And I know one day you will leave me as mother has left me.

I will stand over another goodbye box
The geese will rage beside the moon.
The books will grow inside the trees

And I will kneel close enough
To pick the hair from your chin.
Not yet.

Not today because your pockets are filled with peanuts.
You are making a jelly sandwich and spilling laughter
Into my throat—

Filling me the way a thousand thrushes fill a chimney. ◇

Up North Somewhere

Raymond Philip Asaph

PRETENDING TO BE UNMOVED BY THE BEAUTY SURROUNDING US, I clung to my bad-ass persona like a jacket. We were up north somewhere, near Canada, our truck perched on the ridge of a mountain. Above our truck and the log cabin we were parked beside was the universe, all that blackness and the ancient stars.

The job had been a marathon, nineteen hours from start to finish. With our coats zipped to our throats, we were smoking the day's last cigarettes, me and Stump. We called him that because he had no neck, but this nickname was also a perfect fit for his personality. Sharing only exhaustion, we sat in silence a body-width apart like those long-married old folks you sometimes see in diners. I listened to the rumbling motor, the hum of the heater, until I could no longer bear my loneliness.

"You know what Nietzsche said?" I asked.

"I don't give a shit," he replied.

Stump sucked his cigarette, his face glowing like a jack-o'-lantern.

"He said that which doesn't kill you makes you strong."

"Tell Nietzsche he can go fuck himself."

Right in front of us, just beyond the dashboard, was the vast darkness and a steep drop. There was a river down there; you could sense it flowing by like the Tao. But even during the daylight I'd felt leery about stepping to the very edge for a look. High places sometimes seemed too risky, too tempting.

"You know what else he said?" I asked. "*God is dead.* That was his most famous saying. But *Nietzsche* is dead; so I guess God won *that* argument, huh?"

"You're never gonna get a girlfriend," he told me, though he seemed to be speaking to the windshield.

The couple we had just finished moving, the Wilsons, had said adios forever to Long Island. No more traffic jams and stuck-up attitudes for them. Two people with the hearts of pioneers and the heads of hippies, they had chosen to back out of civilization, a move that I had made only in my dreams. And any couple who could live alone together on a mountain had to be a couple who shared real love, the deepest-running dream of all my life.

"I like these people," I said.

"You like everybody."

"Not true. I don't like you. And I'm never taking another trip with you. You're the heart of fucking darkness and you don't like anybody."

"That's right," he said. "But I'm honest about it."

"Yes." I nodded my heavy head. "That's something."

It was too dark, too dangerous, to drive a truck down a ragged mountain road, so the people were letting us camp out on their property. Thanksgiving was just behind us, Christmas, just ahead; and because some folks tend to be generous round the holidays, I'd thought they might invite us in, let us crash on their couches in front of the wood-burning stove. But in the end, they must have decided we were their moving men, two laborers who, only yesterday, were completely unknown to them. I understood and respected their common sense. Stories of psychopaths filled the newspapers every day. They were very friendly, though; so I was still counting on a big free breakfast in the morning to shake off the cold before the long ride home.

Mrs. Wilson, a strawberry blonde who didn't mind wrinkles, had just said goodnight to us and gone inside to join her husband in bed. At least a foot taller than his wife and stooped like a sunflower, Mr. Wilson had chucked all his suits and ties, turning his curved back on a cubicle in an accounting firm.

"To work the earth with my hands and feel clean," he'd informed me.

"Congratulations," I'd said, giving him a clap on his chicken-bone shoulder. "You got yourself back to the garden."

"Yes, yes, that's it," he'd replied.

Good thing Mr. Wilson had bailed out of business. Nobody goose-stepping through the halls of any corporation was ever going to get him, this long-necked bird with spectacles, who chatted away about ideals and intangibles as we carried his stuff up a rocky path.

"Feels like I'm listening to a boy scout," Stump had mumbled.

"Let's hope he doesn't try to talk to any bears," I'd whispered back.

Of the two, Mrs. Wilson, formerly a nursery-school teacher, reached in deeper. She was patient and pleasant, as uncontrived as a pine cone, and something she had said earlier in the day still filled the spaces inside me. She had called this place, "our slice of paradise."

She was referring to herself and her husband, of course. It was their slice, not mine, but somehow I'd felt included. Her tone had been so sincere and expansive that I'd repeated the phrase with the feeling of a prayer as I took big gulps of air like ice water and exhaled steam that seemed as bold as smoke. Pretty soon, I'd convinced myself that it was my slice of paradise too. And in a way, it was, if only for this one day. But now that the day was over, I felt ripped off. By him, my least favorite coworker, a guy whose only sensitivity was in his teeth.

It should've been different. I was far from home, so all my troubles seemed temporarily suspended or like objects left behind in half-packed cartons, but I was with the wrong person, so I couldn't be free. Stump, this blob of negativity beside me, was the reason paradise was ruined. He was like a cigarette stamped out on a slice of pizza—my slice. And so I mildly despised his disgusting guts.

"I'm sleeping across the front seat with my boots off and the heater blasting," he announced near the end of our smokes, "and you're sleeping out in the box."

That's what we call the back of a truck—the box.

"Good luck not freezing to death," he added. "And if you wake me up in the morning chanting Om, I'm gonna rap you in the skull with a tire iron."

"This is why I haven't killed you yet," I said. "Your sense of humor. You're the most miserable human being I've ever worked with, but you make me giggle. And that's the only thing that kept me from shoving you off this cliff."

"Out," he told me. "Time for my beauty rest."

I dropped my cigarette into a half-bottle of soda, put the cap back on, gave it a shake, dropped the bottle on the floor, opened the door, and stepped down onto the uneven ground. My eyeballs watered immediately. The wind came straight through my clothes. Then a whiff of wood smoke came through the icy air and I had the sense that time, in the form of clocks and calendars, was just another of our human illusions. Looking up and around, I felt immersed in the cosmos. And then I realized I was.

"Close the door!" Stump shouted. I glanced at his shadowed figure behind the wheel. He shrugged like a little boy. "You're making me chilly."

"Man, if you and I ever got stranded up here and started starving, I'd chase you down with a rock and cook you on a campfire."

"No, you wouldn't," he replied. "You'd wait, and I'd kill you first."

I slammed the door with all my love and headed for bed. Touching the truck for balance, which felt like a block of ice, I carefully stepped beside it, trying not to twist my ankle on any roots or rocks. At the open side door, I heaved myself up into the blackness and felt my way to a stack of furniture pads. In no time at all, I was wrapped up like a mummy under a pile of them and counting on my breath to warm me up.

Damn, I thought when my teeth started chattering. *How the hell did cave-people make it through the winters?*

Sleeping in the box was an experience I usually enjoyed because it gave me a kick like camping and a feeling of freedom from all the bullshit we call the real world. But this night was not like any other. My thinking quickly became disjointed and there soon seemed no difference between the cold out there and the cold within.

The snot under my runny nose turned icy. Then my ribs started trembling uncontrollably. Though I dreaded being closed in, I had to get up and pull the side door shut. No, that wasn't going to be enough. Something was really wrong; my whole body knew it. I needed to wake up the Wilsons and push myself into their cabin.

But now I couldn't move. The machinery of my muscles had ceased to function. An immense density pinned me to the floor. I became an animal afraid to die. I started praying, begging. I tried to cry for help, but my mouth was incapable of forming words and there was not enough power in my chest for more than a few dull noises which the silence of the wilderness swallowed at once.

The next morning was quite a surprise. I was not a ghost hovering over my own frozen corpse, another heavy burden some other cursing workers would have to pick up and carry off. I was breathing and there-fore still alive. I rounded my lips and blew a plume of steam. Fresh sun-light stained the walls all around me, flat white walls that were scarred everywhere from the ten-thousand things a generation of movers had forced to fit. The box at dawn—it was beautiful. I felt like singing that Cat Stevens song "Morning Has Broken." And because God had given me a second shot, I was going to be a nice guy forever. Even to that prick in the truck.

Probably smiling like the lucky schmuck who'd won the lottery that week, I pushed the heavy mountain of pads off my body. But just as I was blinking and thinking about firing up my first cigarette, I realized I was not alone. One can sense another's presence. What was near me now was not human, that I knew. And when I turned my head, I saw it, only a few feet from the door—a deer.

It was the one without antlers, the female, the doe, so I scratched my chest through my coat and said, "Hi, I'm Phil."

Her head swung up at once and she held herself very still, studying me sideways with one of her huge brown eyes. I felt flattered as a human being and became aware of the accelerated beating of my heart.

"You sure got some gorgeous eyelashes," I told her. "And those ears—cute as can be, especially when you flick 'em."

She did not respond. Not even a snort. And now I was looking down at the fur of her chest and then across her strong flank, and suddenly everything in me was soft. Not a callus anywhere. An impulse came over me to inch my way over to the edge of the truck and hold out my hand like Saint Francis. But the moment I moved, she moved. Turning her head first, and then her whole body, she wandered out of my line of vision. I crawled to the door, but when I stuck out my head, she was gone–hoof-prints in the frosted grass. Even so, I felt as if she had become a part of me and that I was part of this: nature, the real, real world. All around me was the mountain and a low-floating mist. Something within me felt deeply healed, but I also needed to pee very badly.

Yawning happily, I was soon urinating off the side of the truck. I felt invigorated, natural, at one with all the creatures whose lives leave stains on the earth. And then I felt hungry. Pancakes popped into mind. I narrowed my eyes at the Wilsons' cabin. The chimney was smoking as peacefully as a pipe.

These are exactly the kind of people, I thought, *most likely to have real maple syrup.*

I jumped down from the truck to rouse my driver so we could knock on the front door together. Two hungry faces had more power than one and now that I wasn't dead, I wanted my breakfast. Never would I mention my encounter with the deer. Not to Stump. Some things were just too fragile to share with somebody who wouldn't know how to handle them. Getting food, though, especially free food, was something any animal could grasp. Heading tentatively toward the edge of the cliff, I pounded on the window of the truck as I passed it.

"Sleeping Beauty," I yelled, "wake up!"

Stump sprang up behind the wheel, emitting a litany of curses. His cap was cocked and the hair on one side of his head was flat. Even his mother at that moment would have secretly thought, *My God, this child is ugly.* Why lie? He was. But he wasn't the worst driver in the world. He didn't steal his helper's tips. And he did make you laugh. And sometimes a coworker who makes you laugh is worth more than one who does his share of the work.

"Mrs. Wilson told me she wants to make us pancakes in paradise,"

I said. "So get your ass up and start faking some manners."

At the front of the truck, I got a good grip on the bumper. Then I made sure that both the ground and my footing were secure. No way was I going back to the land of stripmalls and traffic jams without getting a look at this river. Hanging by one arm, I leaned out over the cliff and when I twisted my neck downward, I caught a glimpse of it, a scribble of blue far below.

Stump hit the horn. I snapped back, breathless, my legs quaking. I'd almost just died, twice, before breakfast.

"Hey, we got a long ride home together," I told him. "Let's make it work."

He was probably smirking like a psychopath, maybe even giving me the finger, but I had already turned to sniff the air. Yes, that was the smell of coffee there and coffee made all things possible. I motioned him to follow and started up the path to the cabin, smiling at the thought of breakfast with the Wilsons and still carrying the deer inside me. ◇

The Passing of Multitudes

Meredith Trede

Just a sliver of prairie abuts
this arts haven. Aside from
a scattering of rabbits, the likely

local four-legged fauna
are standard poodles and King
Charles spaniels. Rare, bitter winter,

bald eagles soar by, en route
to fish the great, once-icebound lake,
their sky-darkening Passenger Pigeon

prey long gone. More naturalists
than indigenes prowl the grasslands.
Inside, where preserving food and humans,

through breath-stealing cold,
was winter's main work, images
and words are fed onto blank pages.

The certitude that art survives
the ages: tempered by unanswered
owl call and the tenuous hold of the plains. ◇

Summer Storm

Meredith Trede

Falling asleep, the monotony of rain, rain, rain—
waking to hear the creek's trickle, lulling
gurgle, not this rush, race, grumble

of storm surge pushing water over the car's
hubcaps, up the porch. Get out. Get out.
Crash and tangle of branch and root

battering the crumbling banks. Mounds of baled
hay in white shrink-wrapped covers bobbing
in swollen muddy water, marshmallows

in a flood of hot chocolate. Good-bye hydrangea.
Good-bye trellis, swing, stairs, screen door.
The car sputter-starts, skids us away. ◇

The War against the Ants

James H. Zorn

A T THE BASE OF THE PINE TREE OFF OUR TERRACE, A COLONY OF ants had established their home. It was the summer of 1965. The Marines had landed at Danang that spring. I was nine years old. I had seen the ants, of course: nothing went down in that yard that escaped me. Their parapets had grown from humble ramparts at the beginning of July into a civilization worthy of note by the first of August as they ploughed the sandy earth around the sticky roots of the tree. They were a tiny red species, hardly bigger than the point of a pencil. They could sting, I knew, but I didn't hold this trifling defense against them. The ants were a wonder, full of energy and terrible mystery.

One day, my father saw me squatting by the tree and came to investigate. By now, the ants had expanded their mound into an undulating dune that covered most of the roots. This, I discovered, was unacceptable. I had not thought of the ants as a problem before. Now, I saw that it was good that I had been observing them. What I had thought of as mere wonder turned out to have been a prescient act of surveillance. "Are there more beds like this?" There were none. I felt pleased that my knowledge of the terrain had been recognized, like a seasoned Indian scout's.

My father knew what to do. He led me into the garage, where he poured a measured dose of the gasoline that usually went into the lawn mower into a rusty Maxwell House Coffee can. "You shouldn't use too much," he cautioned. I nodded solemnly: this was a skill I needed for my future, like being able to change a flat tire or handle a bully. I felt betrayed by the ants. All the time I had been watching them, I had assumed them to be a good thing, or at least not a threat. Now I realized that we were the victims, peace-loving propertarians provoked into defending our homeland by unconscionable aggression, morally within our rights. The ants deserved what was coming to them.

My father led the way back to the tree and poured the gasoline, sending most of it straight down the hole. "You have to get them where they live." That made sense to me: take the battle to the enemy. The effect was instantaneous. Walls crumbled and collapsed, hundreds died in the toxic mudflow; and this was only the beginning. There had always been a measure of fear in my wonder at the ants: so like us, and yet so different. In the face of such alienness, everything my father had done, and was about to do, seemed logical and just. He took out a box of matches. "Stand back!" I stepped away, my eyes wide in anticipation. All my life, I had been told not to play with matches, and here was my father about to do just that, but with an elevated purpose, a high adult cause. He lit the match and dropped it into the center of the dark stain of gasoline. The bed exploded into flames. Black smoke fumed toward the sky. Ants raced frantically, curling, singed, facing the doom that had been theirs the moment they dared insert themselves into our yard. God looked down and approved. The ants—communal, strange—died.

My father let the fire burn on for a few minutes, then sprayed it down with the garden hose and went to put away the coffee can. I stood looking at the ruin that had been the ants' world. Here and there, a few scattered survivors dragged themselves away, like Lot's family or Hiroshima victims, through the grass. The bark of the tree was singed black at the base, but the pine stood intact: proud, mighty, piercing the sky, saved by prudent intervention from the ravages of an enemy it did not even know existed.

Over lunch, my father explained the theory behind the attack. If the ants had been allowed to remain, they would have spread beds to other trees, other root systems, and eventually the whole yard might have been contaminated. It was even conceivable that every tree in the yard might have died, not to mention the tender, vulnerable grass. The ants knew no mercy; they did not even have minds. They could not be reasoned with or appeased; there was no negotiation. They had to be stopped, at this tree, now.

I pondered these things over the warm summer days that followed. My existence, which until then had been graced with an innocent unknowing, changed irrevocably. Eternal vigilance was the price of freedom, I now realized. The world was divided into good and evil, humans and ants. I scrutinized the burned-out bed with acuity: the ants must not be permitted to return and rebuild their civilization. Where I had once been an Indian scout, at one with the landscape, I now became an infiltrator, an undercover agent in unfriendly territory.

The ants did not return. Defeated, forewarned, they avoided the no-man's-land at the base of the tree. I patrolled relentlessly, watchful for any sign of a comeback. As the days of summer wore on, the memory of that first engagement faded, but not its lesson.

It was with some sense of triumph, therefore, that I reported to my father two weeks later that the enemy had penetrated the back fence and set up a base about ten feet from the dogwood tree. What astounded me most was the speed with which their land grab had taken place: overnight, as I slept in my bed. If it were not for my daily reconnaissance missions, their putsch might have gone unnoticed for weeks.

My father seemed less impressed by this intelligence than I was, but—perhaps inspired by my enthusiasm—he agreed to another surgical strike. When the moment came, I begged to be the one to pour. "Don't get it on the grass." The matches remained in my father's control.

In the week that followed, I doubled my efforts, expanding my searches beyond the perimeter of the yard. Ants were everywhere, I realized. If we really wanted to stop them, we had to strike at them where they really lived. How long could we just keep waiting for their sneak attacks, their subtle corruptions of our territory? We had to enlarge the war in order to win it.

Across the road, in the sandy grass beside the woods, I found the mother of all ant beds. These ants were not the tiny red kind: these ants were huge, thick as my little finger. Their beds were enormous. The workers had pincers that they used to drag whole grasshoppers down, piecemeal, into their holes to devour. These ants were killers . . . and they lived within walking distance of our home.

I ran to tell my father. This time, he balked. "Those ants aren't bothering anybody. Leave them alone."

I went away, baffled and insecure. Were some ants to be scourged, others ignored? Had he grown so complacent? For days, I fretted. Eventually, I resolved that when the army goes soft at the top, the enlisted men have to take the generalship into their own hands.

I knew the routine: the rusty can, the plastic jug of gasoline for the lawn mower. Matches were easy to find. I set off on my own.

At the site, I found myself hesitant. These ants enjoyed some sort of parental "favored nation" status which I disagreed with, but worried about the consequences of flouting. I sulked, watching them work. They were more interesting than the tiny red species: their beds were solid, compact; a stick driven into the walls sometimes brought out a single, furious worker, the tip of the twig clenched in his jaws. Crouched, watching them, I drifted off into a reverie that was reminiscent of my earlier, innocent days, when the ants and I had been as one.

I was jolted from this by a stinging in my foot. I looked down to see an ant warrior who had found my looming presence over their hunting trails displeasing. Screaming, I jumped away, then cautiously edged back. The ant had stung me. First blood. This was clearly a case of Just Cause.

My strategy after this point was simple: I would wait by an ant bed, my gas can and matches ready, until I was stung. Then, outraged, and with what I was sure would have been the full mandate of public opinion behind me had anybody known, I would bring down on the ants the vengeance which their aggression had provoked. In this way, I dispatched a half-dozen ant beds over the course of the next two weeks in fiery reprisal. When my parents found out what I was doing, they ordered me to stop, of course. To appease them, I confined my activities to times when they weren't around. Still, they suspected. I was warned absolutely not to play with matches and gasoline again, *ever*, or suffer the consequences.

The war against the ants went into hiatus. The cause was never far from mind: I simply realized that the public, for the moment, had no stomach for the conflict. Every night, I watched Huntley and Brinkley deliver the count of dead and wounded in Vietnam that formed the backdrop of my childhood: five American soldiers, fifty-five Vietnamese; two American soldiers, twenty-eight Vietnamese. In that faraway country, people died like ants.

For weeks, I watched a particular bed grow next to the woods beside the road. The insult of their presence ate at me. Their bed was large. Surly with parental protection, they consumed tracts of land that I had previously rendered ant-free. Clearly, this state of affairs could not be allowed to continue.

My chance came. My parents were going out for an hour. I begged to stay at home. The car drove away and I readied my equipment.

Did the ants sense my coming? Had they, in prophecies etched in chemical traces on the walls of their myriad tunnels, foretold this day? This was to be the final battle, the Armageddon that spelled my defeat and eventual—let us hope!—redemption: for I have spent my whole life since then trying to get back, in whatever paltry measure is meted out to adults, that state of innocence in which nothing was my enemy, before my father taught me of the war against the ants.

I stood beside the ant bed, my matches and gasoline in my hands. There was no time to wait for the usual act of provocation. I spread gas in a tight circle around the bed to catch those who might try to escape. There was gas left in the coffee can; in my haste, I had taken too much. With a trembling hand, I lit the match. The flames ignited. Valiantly, heroically, the ants struggled to escape. The capacity for pity which had been mine a few weeks before had not returned to me yet. I watched their agonies in fascination and excitement.

The sound of wheels on gravel in the driveway made me turn. I saw my parents' green station wagon, returning early. In desperation, I threw the incriminating evidence, the can of gas, deep into the woods. A trail of gasoline followed it from the burning bed, the flames igniting the dry, tender leaves and succulent palmetto branches, fanned by a warm August wind. As the conflagration spread toward my neighbors' houses, I stood paralyzed with terror and shame at what I had done. ◇

Ilex

Fred Yannantuono

As jeweler, I live in the adamantine—
naked planes, polished edging, facets
branching like fractals, cold and inexact.

Our holly tree when I was young—
how etched and symmetrical, how knife-like
the spines, how black the green leaves,
each an iron icon of Christmas.

It grew outside the glass I put the loupe to.
Stoic in the wind, unbowed as opal,
its berries the pearls of squirrels.

It caught a fire blight—its leafy rivière
caked in soot. Come spring, the gardener
cut it down, hauling its taproot out with a winch,
replacing it with a much hardier laurel. ◇

Tenure

Fred Yannantuono

It comes with the turf, you say,
this chute from the land of light
to the humid undergrowth, this
mouth to ear, mouth to ear. And
if in unison the caw of a hundred
crows marks the slow, persistent
track of worms through soil, who
is to say who drives whom?

I don't know the facts, so
I plow fields boustrophedon.
I can no more know the truth
than to shower you with gold.
Does the moving mouth in the soil
demand the caw of crows?
Will it inch on in the night
toward a softer inconsistence?
Will a firm, declining rain
draw them through the roots? ◇

Haley and the Enchanted Meadow

Michael Malone

"**M**MMEHEHEMMM."

It's the resonant throat-clearing of a big man, which Mr. Snow certainly is. We're at Gotham, a place off Fifth Avenue that I'd never in a million years be able to afford. But, if Haley's folks are buying, well, I'm game.

"So," starts Mr. Snow. He's got slicked-back hair that's surprisingly dark for a man his age, which appears to be around sixty. Haley told me he played basketball at Columbia, back when Columbia was a national power, and white guys dominated college ball. Mr. Snow looks like he could still post up and go strong to the hole—or chase down and pummel the boy who screwed over his daughter—if need be. He's some high-powered entertainment lawyer; I've seen his name in the gossip pages.

"Haley tells me you went to NYU," says Mr. Snow.

I'm about to correct him, then realize it's probably what I told Haley.

"Uh, yes, sir," I say in a voice I reserve for job interviews, answering summonses, and meeting girlfriends' parents. "NYU. Not far from here."

"We used to play 'em in basketball," he says. "Believe it or not, both NYU and Columbia, where I attended, were among the strongest basketball schools in the nation."

"No kidding," I say. "Academics have certainly surpassed athletics at both institutions."

"Indeed."

"Haley says you're in publishing," says Mrs. Snow.

"Yes, ma'am," I say. "I'm an editor at a wine magazine, writing features about, well, wine—wine expos, wine country, and wine people, and overseeing a wine review."

I don't elaborate; my job sounds more interesting the less I say about it. And I leave "associate" out of my title. I edit. Therefore, I'm an editor. Actually, if you're to boil my job down, I'm a typist: I rewrite press releases for winemakers that advertise in our magazine. More accurately, I give the releases to our intern, Becky, and then cruise job Web sites and dream about a better tomorrow. I'm always nice to Becky, because she's smarter than I am, and I realize that my brighter tomorrow might possibly be linked to her.

"*Wine Enthusiast?*" asks Mr. Snow.

"No . . . "

"*Wine Spectator?*" guesses Mrs. Snow.

"No, the other one, actually."

"I didn't know there was another one," says Mrs. Snow.

"Yup. *Cork & Bottle*," I say. "We're a little younger and less stuffy than the others."

By less stuffy, I mean less advertising.

"And I've written a few children's books as well," I add. They look at each other and agree on a forced smile; they seem to like the wine magazine better than my Honey Bunny series. No problem.

"Interesting," says Mr. Snow. Mrs. Snow, who has streaks of silver in her straight blonde mane, nods in agreement. They're a classic middle-aged New York couple: attractive, well-dressed, with an air of culture and wealth about them. He looks like he's been to more than one party at the Dakota, and she looks like she's got a funny Woody Allen story.

"I've never met a Declan before," says Mrs. Snow. "Am I saying it right?"

"Yes, ma'am. There aren't many of us."

"That's Irish?" she asks.

"Yes. Irish mom, English dad."

"That's uncommon."

"Yes, well, they didn't get along, as you might guess."

"And where do they live?"

"Uh, Mom's here in the city, Dad's probably . . . I'm actually not sure."

There's an awkward silence, as everyone sifts through my family's dirty laundry.

"So, where's the world's best wine made?" Mr. Snow asks. It's the one question I'm asked every time someone finds out what I do for work. I press PLAY on autopilot.

"Well, Mr. Snow, there's always France, of course. And I like what they're doing down in the Southern Hemisphere, most notably South Africa and Australia, what with their Shiraz/Syrah, and they've got a nice array of Cabernets as well. Honestly, though . . . "

This part I love.

" . . . I've had California wines that are every bit as good as the rest of the world's. The Mondavi Cabernet always scores in the 90s, Benziger out of Sonoma makes a terrific Cab Sav-Merlot blend, and I just tried a Concannon Pinot Noir that was sublime—and retails for like fifteen bucks."

Americans are always elated to hear that the U.S. of A. is competing with, even surpassing, the rest of the world. Reds, whites, and blue. Mr. Snow gives a satisfied nod and Mrs. Snow pumps her fist. Haley smiles at me. It's going well. Next they'll ask me to select the wine.

"Well, I guess we'll have to insist you choose our dinner wine," says Mrs. Snow with a smile. "It'd be a shame not to use a resource like you."

I beam. I'm a resource!

The waiter breezes through the specials. There's a pumpkin ravioli in pesto and pine nuts, and a penne with salmon and lots of other things that sound good, especially with the Snows paying.

Haley squeezes my knee under the table. She's got on a sleeveless black turtleneck and a long black skirt. It's a lot of black, and on some girls it might look morose or Goth, but on Haley, offset by her long, straight, blonde hair, fanning out at her shoulders like a veil, it looks wonderful. She was nervous about asking me to meet her folks, and seemed so surprised when I agreed to come along. I told her she was selling me short, measuring me up against a guy stereotype she got from sit-coms. Of course I'd like to go for a free meal at Gotham. Of course I'd like to see the creatures that house the DNA from which she was spawned. And yes, I'm ready to admit to her, her folks and, most importantly, myself, that I'm willing to take this next step in our relationship.

And maybe we'll finally have sex.

I order a bottle of Jekel, out of Monterey, from 1995. It was a good year, I tell them, then wonder if I fared as well that year as the Northern California vineyards did.

"She had all this energy as a kid," says Mrs. Snow, who, after three glasses of Cabernet, has requested I call her Lydia. So I do. We're at the stage of the dinner where they're telling stories about Haley's childhood, much to her mortification. Of course, I fan the flames with probing questions, about her bad haircuts, Shaun Cassidy fetish, and things she had irrational fears of as a kid: shopping carts, a purple frog rocking toy on a playground near their Upper East Side apartment.

"I swear, she'd just fly about the living room, crashing into things. That's why we called her 'Haley,'" says Mr. Snow. "She was like a comet. Still is."

"That's where the name came from?" I ask with genuine surprise. "I thought . . . "

I don't want to say I thought Haley was her given name, even though I'm shocked to hear it's not.

"I thought it was a college nickname."

"I never told you?" asks Haley.

"Nah," I say. "Never. So what's your real name?"

There's a moment of silence; each of the three Snows figures the other one will tell the story. None does.

"Meadow," spits Haley finally.

"Meadow!" I exclaim with much more vigor than I intended. It dawns on me that I've recently attained a fairly serious relationship milestone with a girl named Meadow. I feel so . . . *earthy*.

"Meadow," says Haley, as her parents look bashfully at each other. I'm trying to picture Lydia and Jack Snow in their hippie days—muddy, hirsute, and naked—but I can only muster a vision of them in the uptown urban attire they have on tonight. I can't even picture them outdoors.

"Meadow," I repeat. Maybe it's the Cabernet, but I'm starting to like it.

"Who wants dessert?" asks Meadow.

We all get dessert. I have a flourless chocolate cake, while Meadow gets a raspberry torte. We all order espresso, and drink it at a comfortable pace. I reach for the check, Mr. Snow boxes me out, and then we stand outside the restaurant for a considerable amount of time, making painless small talk on the warm night.

"Well, Declan, it certainly was a pleasure meeting you," says Mrs. Snow.

"Likewise, Lydia," I say, delicately shaking her hand as she leans over for an air kiss.

"Nice meetin' you, Declan," says Mr. Snow in a fraternal, if stern, tone, giving me a firm handshake. "Take care of our Haley, will ya?"

"Yes, sir," I say, flattered to be saddled with the responsibility. I have a vision of me, Haley, and a dog in some house in the woods, seeing the Snows off after a visit. Not sure who's paying the mortgage, but hell, dare to dream.

"Thank you again for dinner," I say.

Mrs. gives a final wave as Mr. flags down a cab.

WE'RE WALKING DOWN TENTH STREET, back to Haley's place. It's a beautiful block—townhouses, carriage houses, places with huge windows that taunt everyone on the street who lives in a rent-stabilized tenement in a shitty project on Avenue A.

Walking hand in hand, neither one of us is speaking, but it doesn't feel awkward. Dinner with Haley's folks has gone really well, no doubt about it. Haley clears her throat and I know what she's gonna say, something like, "Well, that went well."

"Eleanor Roosevelt lived there," says Haley, pointing to a gorgeous brick townhouse with a stable door.

"Really?" I say, scanning my brain for any facts I might have about her that I can bring up. Married to a crippled president, face like a horse. Neither is worth sharing.

"Yup. After FDR died," says Haley. "Supposedly she had a gay lover living with her."

"No shit?" I say. "Really?"

"You won't see it confirmed anywhere," Haley says, "but it was common knowledge. The press left those things alone back then."

I try to picture the Post exhibiting such restraint.

"Well . . . " starts Haley.

"That went well!" I blurt, smiling and giving her hand a squeeze.

"Yes, it did. I'm glad."

"Me too," I say, leading her toward Sixth Avenue.

"TAKE YOUR SHOES OFF," Haley says from the kitchen as I sit on her black-leather couch. She's got Ethan Allen, and I'm just graduating to IKEA. The significance of the shoe-removal command is not lost on me; I've never been invited to take my shoes off at Haley's before. I have a flash of anxiety as I consider the state of my socks—there was little to no forethought as I dressed this morning. I examine them and they thankfully appear OK.

Haley's got a classic West Village one-bedroom, an old walk-up on a block with lots of trees; it's how I picture Paris. She's got exposed brick on one living room wall and a fireplace that doesn't work, but just sits there like an open mouth that can't speak. Her hardwood floors are shiny, with a white throw rug in the middle. There's a dark wood coffee table in the middle of the living room, and on it is a book entitled *The Girl's Guide to Hunting and Fishing*. I had no idea she was such an outdoorsperson, my little Meadow.

A purple candle makes flickering shapes along a white wall, and she's put on some trippy jazz that's either Miles Davis or John Coltrane.

I have no idea which because I don't like jazz. She comes back from the kitchen with two glasses of wine, and hands one to me.

"I didn't know you knew so much about wine," she says.

"I, uh, I know how to stretch my limited knowledge out pretty good."

"Well, it was very impressive."

"Thank you."

"I got you a gift," she says.

"C'mon!"

"Something small."

"What for?"

"No reason," she says. "Just a little gift."

I feel bad for not getting her anything, but how was I to know we were exchanging gifts? She opens the drawer of the end table and pulls out what can only be a CD, wrapped in shiny silver paper.

"Thank you, Hale," I say.

"Open it!"

I do, and see Keanu Reeves in a football uniform, kissing some girl. It's the soundtrack for a movie called "The Replacements."

"It's that band you like!" she gushes. "From Minneapolis. The song about St. Mark's Place!"

"Ri-i-i-ight," I say, turning it over. There's a song by Young MC and a bunch of other stuff by hip hop-sounding acts I never heard of.

"Thanks," I say, leaning over to kiss her. "You're very kind."

"No problem," she says. "Maybe you can burn it for me."

"Sure . . . Meadow," I say, and she recoils slightly.

"No," protests Haley.

"No more Meadow?"

"'Fraid not."

"My new Honey Bunny book takes place in what I've titled *The Enchanted Meadow*," I say. "Coincidence, huh?"

"I'm surprised you didn't make a joke about the daughter on 'The Sopranos,'" says Haley.

"Whyzat?"

"Her name is Meadow."

"I don't have HBO," I say. "I must say, though, I'm a little surprised by the name. I mean, your parents just don't seem like the types to name a kid Meadow. What's your sister's name, Forest?"

Haley takes a sip of her wine, which sends a flush of color throughout her pleasantly pale face. There's a pause, and I know she's hiding something. I prod her with a nod.

"Brooke," she mumbles.

"C'mon."

"I'm serious, Declan," she says, giving me a look that reinforces the statement. "I wish I was kidding. *God,* I wish I was kidding."

"Brooke!" I exclaim.

"Yup. And she's still a Brooke. At least I had the good sense to run around like a lunatic and get a nickname."

"Brooke and Meadow," I state. "That . . . just . . . blows my mind."

"I know, I know. It's . . . fucked up."

Haley never curses. The swear sticks out like a wine stain on her white throw rug.

"Like I said, I just don't see your parents as the hippie types."

"They're not," says Meadow, who I promise I'm calling Meadow for the last time.

"I sense a story coming on."

"I'd rather not," says Haley. "Maybe when I know you better."

There's a flirty tone to her protestations, so I lean over and kiss her.

"I met your parents . . . "

"You really wanna know?"

"Yup."

"It's fucking stupid."

Apparently Haley only curses when talking about her family's fucked-up, fucking stupid names.

"Go on," I say. "I'll tell you something stupid about me."

"Okay." She laughs, taking a healthy slug of wine and beginning the story. "When my parents were first married, they had no money."

"They look like they were born rich."

"Yeah, they play the game well," explains Haley. "Sort of like you and your wine. Anyway, for the first few years they were married, they had this crappy little apartment out in Long Island. Sorry, on Long Island—my dad always corrects me. It was my grandmother's house, and they rented the basement. The ceiling was about six feet high, and my dad's, ya know, a pretty big guy, even bigger then. I went back to see the place once. It was pretty heinous.

"My dad was working in the city," she continues, "as a runner on Wall Street."

"Runner?"

"Lowest life form in the business. You literally run around and place orders for brokers."

"Ouch."

"Yeah," she says. "A real bottom feeder. He was doing that and going to law school, and my mom was teaching. My dad would get home late, and Mom had to get up early, so they didn't have much time for each other. But almost every night when it was warm, they'd get into my dad's old car and drive down to Jones Beach. Back then, they didn't have any kind of security there, and you could just sort of walk onto the beach. My dad didn't get home till ten or so, and there wasn't usually anyone there by the time they got there, so they'd throw a blanket down and—"

"Screw," I blurt. I'm an idiot.

"No," laughs Haley. "Well, maybe. I never thought about it."

Obviously, it was the first thing *I* thought about.

"So they'd hang out there every night. Once they had me and my sister, they never really got much of a chance to go back, at least not on their own. And after my dad started moving up and making, ya know, more money, they bought a place in the city. He became an attorney and that was the end of their quiet nights of watching the waves."

"Nice," I say, and it does sound nice. It's a nice story.

But wait. It's not over. It can't be over. Something's missing.

"What about the names?"

"Oh!" says Haley. "I almost forgot. This is the stupid part. They used to take the Meadowbrook Parkway to the beach. And those nights were always such special memories for them. So I got Meadow, and Brooke got Brooke."

"Wow," I say. "So they *were* screwing on the beach."

"Maybe," says Haley.

I'm with someone sharing a name with a highway. I have something in common with Haley's neighbor, Eleanor Roosevelt.

"You should get a toll-free ride every time you're on the Meadowbrook," I suggest lamely. She laughs anyway.

"It's free for everyone," she says.

"Well . . . you should get your own lane, or something."

"I'm not on the Meadowbrook very often."

"Maybe we'll take a ride out there when it gets warmer," I say, unsure how I suddenly seem to have access to an automobile. "Go to the beach."

"That sounds wonderful," says Haley, putting her wine on the coffee table and resting her head against my chest.

I can smell the ocean in her hair.

Miles or Coltrane is wailing away, positively *wailing*, as Haley turns her head up for a kiss, and I like jazz for the first time in my life. And those tunes just go on and on. He's still wailing when we get to our feet a bit later. I don't think Haley's going to call me on sharing something stupid about my life, and I'm grateful for it; it would be hard to pare down my list. I shake a little life into my sleepy limbs and head; this all seems to be happening in a dizzying, surreal fashion. Haley leads me by the hand toward her bedroom, like a tow truck pulling a car with a blown engine . . . on the Meadowbrook. ◇

Narcissus

Catherine Faurot

Who knew the garden-variety daffodil,
Wordsworth's strumpet flower strewn across all those fields,
flashing sunny undersides
                    in your mind's eye and mine—

and her slightly more modest sister, the jonquil—
although that coquette will propagate just
as readily if left untended—

all come from that singular flower,

                    narcissus:

    named for the boy who refused
to fuck, who turned his face to his own face,
a solipsism of one and a watery reflection.

The bulbs we ship already have next year's
flowers set inside them.

                I've chosen
my daffodils carefully. The Pistachio
flower has a pale-green tint, for the *Khloē*

the newness of spring. Its perianth rings
the central corona with decorum.

I'm not desperate—

I hope they spread, multiply with golden
abandon—
        but like the bulbs' namesake,
my own cold refusals set termination
        under my skin. ◇

Bone of
My Bones
(the rib speaks)

Catherine Faurot

What a mockery.

     The wound itself
looks like a woman's miracle mouth,
the red oval slit seeping blood in the very
    first rib cage.

     Words from other mouths
tell the same story: man comes from woman
just as *ish* comes from *ishah* in the mother
tongue,
    not this backward version.

     It hurt, of course—
cleaving along the center line, the heart, through
the mud-colored skin of the Adamah, the earth-
thing that we come from—

not the pasty, wax-museum man you think,
dainty male genitals dangling like fruit, but
    Eden's hermaphroditic golem,
    dazzling androgynous angel of clay:

now split—

I

was taken out—what a loss—I
not you, we now a glued-together line
juncture always the point of fracture—
    even when we come together
    with the fumbling magnetism
        of the cloven. ◇

The Catherine Wheel

Catherine Faurot

One wrist shackled to the wheel's rim:
the future saint swings, terrible
and unhinged, crimped wrist cut
by the pendulum's arc.

Alas, the kindness—the balance—
of next capturing the opposite ankle
does not occur—
                both left hand
and foot are bound. She flaps
like a scab. She writes with a pen
of gold paint not yet painted.

The wheel, which is time, rolls forward.

Inside the icon's crackled rectangle
her other foot is bound by wires.
Her life ebbs away.
That's what happens. She writes
the whole time. She writes on leaves,

on bark: on the dark road of childhood
heady with the scent of dirt.

Finally she clamps
the last free hand down with her own
golden thread.
      She rolls and rolls—
taut, ecstatic. ◇

The Nosebleed Kid

Katherine Blaine Hurley

THE NOSE TAMPON WORRIED GLADYS THE LEAST.

Gladys—a pudgy girl by nature and fat by skill—sat on the bleachers, watching the other girls run laps around the gym. The freshmen at St. Bartholomew's Church of the Holy Benediction and School for Girls bounced in their matching gym uniforms: green shorts, white shirts, about half of them filled with boobs. Gladys counted how many as she pulled at the tampon string dangling from her right nostril. In her left was the other half of the tampon, cut by the school nurse. Both were stuffy in Gladys's nose, which she twitched as she fingered the string.

"Gladys, stop pulling on that thing!" Mrs. Crolin yelled from center court, where she stood newly infamous in her matching maroon sweat suit. Mrs. Crolin had decided to dress up for the occasion, her last day at St. Bartholomew's, and to make the girls remember an important lesson regarding the spreading of gossip about their gym teacher.

"Keep it moving, Dolphins!" Mrs. Crolin yelled at the dozen girls running in a perfectly spaced line, all but Machine Gun Margaret, who pumped her arms furiously a turn behind.

"Machine Gun, move those legs like you move your mouth!" Mrs. Crolin shouted as she straddled the cartoon dolphin painted on the medallion of center court, one foot in its winking eye, the other in its blowhole.

Machine Gun tried, pumping the poorly greased pistons of her arms like a toy locomotive that's been lifted from the tracks. The pack of Dolphins took off without her.

Gladys watched as the girls passed. She pulled at the cotton string absentmindedly, her eyes fixed on Hannah Russo and the other soccer girls, who glided effortlessly around the black outline of the basketball court. Every girl needed to play a sport at St. Batholomew's. She had to wear the proud Dolphin green on more than just her uniform skirt. Sister Mary O'Donnolly had told them, "Good self-esteem comes from having a number on your back."

Gladys had been on the soccer team for four days until she got cut. Nobody at St. Bartholomew's had ever gotten cut from anything, but due to Gladys's condition and, she believed, her grotesquely visible suffering when she ran back and forth on the soccer field, Coach Sister Veradetta decided to let the poor thing resign and ride out the rest of her athletics requirement as a manager for the basketball team.

Gladys was The Nosebleed Kid, an unfortunate subset of a subset of the reasons to be unpopular in high school. Though kids usually grow out of this unannounced social danger by the second grade, Gladys was Sweet Fourteen and still losing blood. Anything could set her off: dry air, a persistent headcold, too much of anything that made her want to cry. But Gladys didn't cry. She just held it all in there, right up in her nasal passages, until things burst. Waking up every morning was like doing repair work on a Cold War nuclear submarine. Just like that outdated rover of the murky deep, Gladys looked like hardy machinery but was prone to leaks. But mostly, Gladys's nose just bled at whatever time was the most inopportune and kept bleeding and bleeding no matter what advice people gave. Put your head back. Squeeze the bridge. Keep your fingers out of there. The blood just kept flowing after all the advice-givers were gone, and Gladys was left with tissue chunks up her nose, silently counting floor tiles.

But what Gladys worried about most now was her other bleeding. Always *the* kid with the bloody face, The Nosebleed Kid had had another distinction, too. As far as she could tell, Gladys was also the only girl that hadn't had her period—until today that is. It was in that very gym class, in fact, just twenty minutes before, that Gladys had been blessed while she was in the locker room changing into her gym shorts. She saw the bloody spot with horrified confusion: her nosebleed? In her *underpants?*

When she realized her nose was not bleeding, and that it must be that *other* part, she was so ashamed and embarrassed that her nose began bleeding again, too. Then she was stuck there, shorts around her ankles, horrified, leaky, and down so many quarts. That's when she passed out.

When Gladys woke up, Mrs. Crolin was leaning over her with one hand smooshing together both Gladys's cheeks. She shook Gladys's face back and forth.

"Wake up! Wake up," Mrs. Crolin repeated as Jenny Ogalman yelled, "Oh, gross, Mrs. Crolin! Watch out! All that blood from her face!"

Gladys expected to be sent home from school after that, but when Sister Karen Paulino tried to phone Gladys's mother and nobody picked up, Gladys was sent to the school nurse, who set her up with a pad for her lower half and a tampon cut in two for her face.

Sister Maria Excelsior, the ninety-three-year-old nun who worked as school secretary, took Gladys to a back closet and found her a spare uniform that was two sizes too big. She then sent Gladys back to gym class with a note that Mrs. Crolin shoved in her pocket, saying, "Yeah, no shit," and in her baggy uniform, Gladys now sat. On the bleachers. Watching the boobs and uniforms. Bleeding from the face and other parts.

Gladys knew that right now life could be worse. For one, she was finally getting a nosebleed that was beneficial: sitting out of this gym class felt like a gift from the Lord Jesus Christ Himself, to whom Gladys would sometimes pray, like the nuns told her to, but she mostly asked his opinion on stuff. "Lord Jesus Christ, what sweater do you think Jenny Meyers would like the best on me on dress-down day?" Things like that.

"Gladys!" Mrs. Crolin yelled. "You done with the drippy-drip yet?"

Gladys touched the tampon half in her left nostril. It was growing uncomfortably large in her nose.

"No," Gladys answered.

Machine Gun huffed by. A stampede of green and white passed her again.

"Well, stop touching those tampons," Mrs. Crolin said as she brought her whistle to her lips. When she blew, the floor shook with squeaking sneakers.

"One-minute water break!" Mrs. Crolin yelled, smiling, and then corrected herself. "Thirty-second water break."

The soccer girls sprinted toward the locker room. The others walked. And then there was Machine Gun Margaret, collapsed in the far corner. Gladys watched Mrs. Crolin walk like a Wild West sheriff to a gunfight she was already bored of.

"Margaret. Butt. Up." Mrs. Crolin said.

Machine Gun rolled over and pushed herself up like a just-birthed giraffe.

Mrs. Crolin nodded at her watch and secured her whistle first to her lips, then in her teeth. Gladys studied the clench around her jaw. Mrs. Crolin blew hard. The locker room emptied out, green shorts, white shirts exploding in a blur. Mrs. Crolin clapped her hands as the girls took to the line again.

"All period, ladies!" she said. "Indian Run it!"

The whistle blew. The girls were off. Mrs. Crolin smiled as the whistle fell from her lips and bounced on its black string against her sports-bra'd, sweat-shirted chest. Gladys pressed her thumb against the tampon in her nostril, pulled her thumb away to see if it had left a little blood stamp. It had. Then something much more interesting caught her eye.

Hannah Russo, at the back of the line this time, broke from the pack. She sprinted past a dozen girls, and Gladys snorted. She imagined Hannah looking at her the way she had that day on the soccer field, and then she chastised herself, imagined snorting up her tampon right there as she sat on the bleachers, imagined herself violently coughing as Mrs. Crolin came over and Heimliched it out. She imagined the doughy red wad landing at Hannah's feet like Gladys's own heart, and she imagined Hannah giving it a quick punt as she overtook the line and became Indian lead.

THE INDIAN RUN—along with what everyone at St. Bartholomew's Church of the Holy Benediction and School for Girls identifies as a racist but athletically approved name—is a masochistic design of circular torture in which the only instrument of destruction is one's own feet. Just ask Machine Gun Margaret. "It's the worst, most terrible, awful thing that can ever happen to you, ever, ever, ever, ever, ever," Margaret will say.

Everyone runs in a line with the last person racing up to try to become the first person in line. Once she catches up and becomes first, the current person in last place races up the line to overtake *that* person in first. In theory, it should be a smooth, basically biblical transition, the last becoming first and what-have-you. This being said, if you're very fast, you catch up to the front of the line right away. If you are not very fast and the person in the front is *a total asshole* and not nice enough to slow down, you could be chasing that line for the rest of your natural life.

Mrs. Crolin knew all about fast little assholes and that's why the Lady Dolphins were running Indian Runs all day, in every gym class, due to a little celebratory going-away party Mrs. Crolin was throwing for herself. Some of the girls suspected they were being punished for the charming little cheer they had chanted, but none of them could be sure. Mrs. Crolin said nothing to their questions, just "Indian Run! All day!" and watched, smiling to herself, as these sprightly little beauties, who had taken a very private moment and turned it into a very public ordeal, ran around and around and around again.

She had been fighting with her husband, that much Mrs. Crolin was willing to admit when the directress had asked, and he had, in fact, slammed the front of his Volvo into the back of her Subaru in the tennis parking lot—that much anyone who was at tennis practice could attest to as well. He had come to finish a fight that had started that morning and continued via text all day. Mrs. Crolin was coaching tennis practice when her husband pulled into the parking lot in that dramatic fashion and marched up to the fence.

Mrs. Crolin told the girls to go for a run, away from the tennis courts, down to the soccer fields. The team of curious girls took off very, very slowly, with Anna Clark stopping to get her camera phone surreptitiously from her bag as she jogged by it.

Anna didn't catch much footage except some bouncing elbows and murmured "Ooo, he looks pissed," and "That woman's *married?*" on the first pass. But when the girls looped back toward the courts on their second lap, she caught this:

"Because I'm a lesbian, Phillip! Because I'm an L-E-esbian!" Mrs. Crolin screamed, her fingers interlaced in the fence, pulling back on the links. Mr. Crolin yelled back a few choice things, too, on the other side of that fence, but nobody remembers them. The part that became an Internet sensation was Mrs. Crolin's chant in the face of marital adversity: "L-E-S, Phillip! B-, Phillip! I-A-N, Phillip!" It was watched some ten thousand times by the students and other discrete Web viewers who had chanced upon "Coach Goes CRAZY For Lesbians!!!" through various search terms.

When the school caught wind of the video and had Anna Clark take it down, Mrs. Crolin thought the whole issue would die down. The Sisters of Mercy at St. Bartholomew's were known for their compassion and progressiveness. When the directress, Sister Mary Michael Jude, called Mrs. Crolin into her office the next day, she said, "I would be willing to forget this entire unfortunate incident except . . . "

Then she opened her office door and the sounds of girls passing through the hallway collected in one unified chant.

"L-E-esbian!" they were singing. "I, Phillip! A, Phillip!"

Sister Mary Michael Jude, a grandmotherly woman who stood no taller than four-foot-six, shut her door. She looked up at Mrs. Crolin, who was looking over the nun's head, eyes fixed on the door's frosted glass.

"We simply cannot have that," Sister Mary Michael Jude said.

GLADYS TWISTED at the wedged cotton in her nostril as she watched

Hannah Russo overtake Becky God Damn Jacobson on the line.

Gladys's first experience with an Indian Run—and Hannah Russo—had taken place just a few months before, during her brief encounter with the soccer team and the outright lie that she had been told by her father on the first day of tryouts: "Just try out for goalie. They never have to run." It took seventeen minutes for Gladys to catch up on that first run. And that seventeen minutes was a gift from Jesus and Hannah Russo.

The girl who had been in front and who happened to be the fastest senior on the St. Bartholomew's Church of the Divine Benediction and School for Girls' soccer team was Becky God Damn Jacobson, who would not slow down for anybody. At sixteen minutes fifty-seven seconds into Gladys's attempt to overtake the group, the soccer coach yelled from the sidelines that Becky had a phone call from her mother that she had to take.

Beautiful Hannah Russo—transfer from St. Gwen's Academy and the most desirable girl on the field, according to proclamations by the boys who would stop to watch at the chain-link fence—had been running right behind Becky God Damn Jacobson. It was Hannah who finally slowed down to a crawl so that sweaty, coughing, dry-heaving Gladys could overtake her. Gladys herself was overtaken as line leader within seven seconds but still she had made it to the front and could rest for those moments as the slowest leader the Indian Run line had ever had. Practice ended before Gladys got to the back of the line again. She dropped like a sack of cement mix when Coach blew her whistle and everyone else headed toward the sidelines to get a drink.

And that's when she saw Hannah Russo touch a slender knuckle to her Roman nose and pull down a little spot of red. Hannah recognized it and opened her mouth to say something, though she couldn't remember what, something stupid like "You're just like me."

But before she could, Hannah sniffed real hard and put that same finger to her lips to shush her, a secret pact. She walked right next to Gladys, who was pushing herself up awkwardly and hurriedly from the ground.

"I wasn't going to tell you to put your head back," Gladys said. She was sounding her most earnest. "No way. That doesn't help. That's the stupid thing everyone says to me, but what I try . . . "

The other girls were starting to look. What was Nosebleed saying to the new girl? They strained to hear.

"That's our little secret," Hannah said in a whisper that went through Gladys's ears, tickled the roof of her mouth, and went up to kiss her brain.

"Our little . . . " Gladys started to repeat.

"All right!" Hannah yelled. "Let's get the fuck back out there!"

"WHAT'S GOING ON?" Mrs. Crolin yelled to Gladys from center court.

Gladys stopped squeezing the edges of her nose. "I'm just . . . "

"You think I don't see everything?" Mrs. Crolin shouted. "Do I have to cut you another tampon?"

Gladys felt the string dangle against her dry mouth. The Indian Run line ran past the bleachers, the girls' breath as heavy as their footsteps, as from the back, Machine Gun Margaret tried to catch up. Hannah Russo slowed down and let Machine Gun Margaret catch up. As soon as she was in second place, Hannah pulled off to the side, panting toward the ceiling, each hand raised high over her head as though she had a cramp. Mrs. Crolin spotted the unscheduled break.

"Miss Russo!" Mrs. Crolin shouted.

Mrs. Crolin turned back to Gladys and waved her hand.

"Gladys, just go fix your nose or whatever you need in the locker room, please." Mrs. Crolin said. "Now, Miss Russo . . . "

Gladys looked once more at Hannah—still eyeing the ceiling, her chest rising and falling, lifting her breasts to a quick beat—before she lumbered down off the bleachers and into the locker room.

On the other side of the gym, the Dolphins ran.

In the locker room mirror, Gladys looked at her distended nose, the red crust around the edges, aggravated by the cotton blocks. Gladys put both her elbows on the countertop around the sink and leaned into the mirror. With her index finger and thumb, she grabbed hold of the remaining tampon half in her left nostril and pulled. It popped out and a rush of fresh air and the smell of mildew-y shower curtains blew in.

Gladys turned her head slightly to the left, keeping her eyes on her nose in the mirror. No blood came out.

She heard the door from the gym swing open. The noise startled Gladys and the blood-soaked tampon fell into the sink. Gladys tried to look around the partition to see who had come in, but felt warmth in her nose again. She turned back to the mirror and saw that her right nostril was bleeding. Underneath that, she saw red droplets on her borrowed uniform shirt. She put her index finger over her nostril.

Hannah Russo walked around the partition and saw Gladys—and her one-finger plug—standing there.

"Oh," Hannah said, pulling back on her heels.

Gladys yanked her finger away from her nostril. It dripped.

"Hi," Gladys said.

"Are you okay?" Hannah said. Sweat was dripping from her forehead down to her temples. Gladys noticed that her cheeks glistened like the freshly washed skin of a nectarine.

"You're bleeding all over your shirt," Hannah said.

Gladys looked down at herself. She counted six healthy red circles of blood on the white oxford shirt. She felt the blood collect again at the bottom of her nose. Gladys jerked her head up and put the heel of her hand to her nostril.

"It'll stop soon," Gladys said.

"Oh," Hannah said. "Okay, good."

Hannah pointed at the bathroom stalls.

"I have to . . . just . . . "

"Oh, sure, sure, of course, sure. Do you want me to leave?" Gladys said.

Hannah smirked.

"No, I don't want you to leave. I don't mind if you stay," Hannah said.

"Well, that's what they're here for," Gladys said, pointing at the stalls and smiling. She wanted to hit herself on the head repeatedly after saying it.

"Yup," Hannah said.

Gladys wished all the blood would drain out of her nose so she'd drop dead on the tiles.

Hannah smiled a little and walked quickly toward the farthest stall.

Gladys watched the door as Hannah closed it behind her. Gladys realized she was staring—at a bathroom door no less! A creep!—and spun around to the sink. She turned the water on and moved her hand away from her face. She rinsed her palm off in the water before dropping her head down into the sink. She shoved her nose into the stream.

"Please stop," she whispered, the water running into her mouth. "Please stop. Please stop. Please stop."

She heard the toilet flush.

Gladys yanked her head out of the sink just as Hannah came out of the stall. Gladys watched in the mirror as Hannah walked toward her, head down, and turned the water on in the sink right next to hers.

Gladys looked down at Hannah's arm next to her own elbow. Her eyes ran to Hannah's hands, wringing together slowly as the suds bubbled up and washed away.

"You should change your shirt," Hannah said. Gladys yanked her eyes back to the mirror. Hannah was still looking down at her own hands.

"They gave me this one," Gladys said. She noticed her nose had stopped bleeding. In fact, her whole face felt completely dried out, as if her eyes might shrink up to nothing, her throat cave in on itself.

"The nuns are nice here," Hannah said. She made eye contact with Gladys in the mirror. "They're not always so nice. I've been to three different Catholic schools before this. They keep . . . "

Gladys nodded, but Hannah didn't go on. While she waited for Hannah to speak again, Gladys checked her nose reflexively—nervously, one nostril at a time—with the back of her index finger. Hannah walked over to the paper-towel dispenser.

"I have another shirt," Hannah said. "I'm—I'm like Mrs. Crolin. I mean, I have a lot of matching shirts."

And with that, she moved close to Gladys and The Nosebleed Kid froze, looking back at Hannah Russo's face so very close to hers. Hannah leaned in and kissed her. Gladys stood there, someone's lips on hers—soft pressure, that's all Gladys remembered feeling, soft pressure. Gladys was afraid to move. She loved it. She was afraid to move. She loved it and was afraid to move.

A mighty gasp rose up like the chorus of angels at God's feet. It echoed off the corner tiles of the bathroom and shower stalls.

Hannah pulled away.

"I know. I shouldn't have, but it's—" she began.

But it was not Gladys who gasped. Watching them kiss, Gladys and Hannah realized as they pulled apart, were five of the fastest girls from the soccer team, their eyebrows contorted, their mouths dangling like a row of country-road mailboxes just opened up.

A moment later, Machine Gun Margaret shoved her wheezing frame through the locker-room door and saw all seven girls standing completely still. The soccer girls, with their backs to her, stood stiff, and Gladys and Hannah, standing strangely close to one another by the sinks, stared wild-eyed back at them.

"Holy, holy, holy, holy shit, shit, shit," Machine Gun Margaret said. "Something happened!"

"Gross!" Becky God Damn Jacobson yelled from where she stood with the other soccer girls. "Gladys, your nose! Hannah, Gladys's nose! Gross!"

The rest of the gym class pushed in through the locker-room door, and started shoving in as best they could to the bathroom section to see what the other girls were looking at. Behind them, Mrs. Crolin emerged, just as Hannah put her head in her hands.

"Why are all of you . . . Hannah, why are you crying?" Mrs. Crolin said.

"They were kissing!" Gracie Costanza said. "Hannah was kissing The Nosebleed Kid!"

The class gasped in unison, with one or two yelling, "Gross!"

Gladys checked her nostrils with the back of her index finger. One quick swipe this time. She looked at Hannah. She wanted to touch her, speak softly to her, ask her to stop crying. And then there was another part of Gladys that wanted to ditch Hannah by running into the showers, crouching in the corner, and hiding behind the mildew-y curtains with her new life partners, the moldy tiles.

And then Mrs. Crolin's voice broke through all of it:

"Oh, for God's sake, the whole world is shit."

She pushed past the girls and stood next to Gladys and Hannah.

"Let people have a moment of happiness."

Mrs. Crolin yanked open the cabinets under the sinks, pulled out two tampons and tossed them both toward Gladys. Gladys caught one and dropped the other. Hannah ran off, pushing past her open-mouthed classmates, sobbing.

Mrs. Crolin shoved past the girls again. They all turned to watch her leave. For a moment, the slamming door as Mrs. Crolin left the locker room was the only sound left licking at the tiles and echoing in their ears.

The crowd of ninth-grade eyes turned back to The Nosebleed Kid. Gladys looked back at them, one tampon in her hand, one at her feet. She felt swallowed in someone else's forgotten uniform. She thought they would crucify her.

Hannah sniffled somewhere in the locker room unseen.

Then two girls broke from the mob and pushed past Gladys. They dove into the sink cabinets behind her.

"Why didn't we ever look in here?" Jessie London asked her fellow scavenger.

The rest of the girls went to their lockers and started to change in front of everyone.

"Hannah . . . " Gladys heard a girl softly say.

"I found soap down here," Ruth Connelly said at Gladys's feet, the top half of her body leaning into the cabinet.

"The good kind!" she said.

Jessie London leaned down to see. She looked at the tampon at Gladys's feet, picked it up, and handed it to Gladys. Jessie dove back down.

"Move over, Ruth," she said, squeezing her body in.

Gladys looked in the mirror. At the edges of her nostril were hints of red. She ran her index finger under her nose and pulled her hand away. There in her palm, she saw the beginnings of a ginormous bleed. ◇

The Oyster Feast

Susan V. Walton

Drawn in from November rain
through glowing arch and doorway
to Sunday embrace at hearthside,
we arrive in the yellow kitchen,
face-to-face with the Oysterman—in
his checkered apron, oyster knife
poised, to indicate trays of gleaming
Wellfleets, platters of Chesapeakes—
pearly sheen of muscle, gills, and mantle,
to lift dark-edged ruffles over miracles
of filtration, inside each sedimentary
shell—green and slim from East Coast
farms, or barnacled and stout
from the brack of the Delmarva.
Stirred by this tableau vivant,
we hear a whirr outdoors,
look up to swarming grackles
deciding with one mind to rise
and dive, lift, hesitate,
then plummet.
More intense than rain, more intent
than tumble of russet leaves,
they come to roost—
a pane of glass apart from us
inside
with the oysters. ◇

How a House Falls Apart

Carlyn Attman

THERE IS A HOLE IN THE ROOF OF MY BUBBY'S HOME. I USED TO SIT under it, when it first appeared—a sky-colored paint drop stuck at the ceiling. I'd watch the clouds shift their shapes over and over again, lion to butterfly to riverwater, through that tiny window. We all noticed it growing quietly, but it was two whole years before we said anything. My Bubby, she tried to point it out, but Zayde kissed her on the lips instead. He said, "Well Mil, how 'bout it?" and took her hand in dance. Eventually one of us lifted a finger toward the ceiling. "You got a skylight now, Mildred? What, the windows weren't good enough for you?"

Everyone laughed, relieved that it was now named.

On Saturday morning we basked under the opening. We marveled that weather could touch our browning bodies while we were still *inside*. The sun warmed the carpets, and my Bubby joked that she could cook the chicken in that midday glow.

I remember one day, staring at that picture of her from when she was seventeen. Young and small-waisted, thick brown hair pinned behind her ears. Her face spread in a country-beauty smile as she turned to the camera, mid-air. What a rider, what a beauty, dancer's legs, my Zayde tells me.

It was then that the rain began to fall. Raindrops spotted the carpet and our hair-dos were coming undone. So we tried, for the first time, to fix the hole. My father, like a hero on his knees, redid the wooden roof, shingle by shingle. But the hole reappeared. So we tried asphalt, and then metal. But the hole came back while the copper was still copper.

It rained and rained and we all bought new coats and threw away the old ones. My sister was glad of it and so was my Bubby. "It's about time I get rid of this *shmatte*," she said, smiling, as she stuffed her old trenchcoat into a bloated trashbag.

The rain rolled down our faces as we tried to light the candles on my Zayde's hanukkia. But all eight hissed into smoke. We sat in the corners, my sister and I, tucked between the sofa and the wall. We played dreidel and bit through the gold foil of our gelt like monsters. Mom and Dad and Bubby and Zayde sat on the couches around us, talking about paper and the state of things as they sipped into merriment.

The water began to rise, higher and higher, filling my stockings and patent-leather shoes. We all had to stand crowded on the coffee table. "Keep playing!" my father shouted at my sister and me, and we did, laughing from the pit between our lungs and our hearts, pushing each other down under the flood. Eventually the soup, simmering on the stove filled with rain and flowed like snakes into the creeping tide. "Dinner's ready!" yelled my Bubby. We all grabbed spoons, fishing in the waters for soggy carrots and onions.

The latkes floated past us with mice at the helms shouting to each other like soldiers. One played a lament on his fiddle as he drowned slowly in a scoop of sour cream.

This is when my mother's eyes broke. She took our hands, mine and my sister's. "We have to leave." My father understood. I grabbed the picture of my Bubby, where she's flying with the horses, and stuffed it in my pocket as I was lifted through the door.

The last I saw, she was twirling in the living room, her coat floating around her in a scarlet ring.

WE CAME BACK the next evening, in new boots, our hair dry. Mine braided down my back. Dad knocked on the door and Zayde opened it, smiling, but did not invite us inside. He said, "Tonight we'll celebrate outdoors!" And I was glad of it because these are the grasses I tangled in my toes when I was younger and happier. Mom and Dad and Zayde went into the house but told the two of us to run around a bit. We found an old maple and leapt between its branches like mouse soldiers leaping between the windows of a burning city.

As they laid down a checkered blanket I saw the moon rise for the first time in my life. It took seven seconds and rippled the sky so that, for a moment, I wasn't sure if I was or wasn't a fish.

"Come, come around, children!" called Zayde and we skipped toward him, our bellies grumbling as children's bellies do. "Kiss Bubby hello," said Father. "Where is she?" I asked. He pointed to an empty space on the left side of my Zayde. I was confused and so I asked my father a second time, "Where is she?" He pointed again and this time I saw her coat. Draped around a sapling. "That's not her. That's just a sapling," I said and my father turned to the fire for a second before telling me in a quiet and violent voice that I was a bad child and would kiss my Bubby at once or no dessert. I wasn't hungry anymore.

Slowly I walked toward the tree, snapping under the garment's weight. I knelt down and scrunched my lips in the air above the branches pretending with all my might that the air was her warm, loose skin. I sucked in only sky but made a convincing sound nonetheless. Everyone nodded in approval. Zayde turned to me, still smiling. A wide grin that reached the tops of his cheeks, bunched together and hopeful like my kissing. His eyes, though, were still, like the porcelain doll he gave me last Hanukkah. It sits on a chair in my room and I cover my head in blankets before sleeping. It was then I saw the cracks in his happy lips—the caked red face paint, split and streaming down his neck on the backs of tears. He was not as good a pretender as I was, but I didn't say anything. I was proud of him for trying.

We made conversation. And watched the fireflies crowd around our bodies. Crickets and cicadas weighted our silences into music. We were all glad of it and breathed in secret recovery. The adults went back inside to gather dessert. My sister and I made up stories about a girl who had wings under her skin and decided, one day, to cut lines in her back and fly into the stars. Then we moved our scapulas in close-eyed flight.

When it was time to say good-bye, the Bubby-tree was broken, bowed into the ground so that her middle was a jagged green notch. I pulled the picture from my pocket, of her on a heaven horse, and unfastened the frame. The paper was yellowed, its edges crumbled under my fingers. I stuck it in the notch where it swayed gracefully against the evening. I kissed her face and said "Thank you for dinner, Bubby! See you soon."

I DIDN'T GO BACK. Not for a long time. Not until I grew out of that new coat and then another and another. My father tried to pull me to that house, but I wouldn't go and I was stronger now and my horses were faster than his feet. I have been to China, Italy, and France. I have brewed hot chocolate on Mount Everest and taken lover after lover in my arms. Told them my stories, turned my teeth black with coffee, then brushed them clean again. I have thought, in the idle moments from breath to breath, about that day we crowded on the table and fished in the rainwater with our silver spoons. Or when I was much younger and she held me against her chest calling me sweet Yiddish names. And I have passionately forgotten the curve of the tree line against the meadow. The smell of her scarves. My feet have holes in them, from walking on fire and dancing on the other side. And I am glad of it.

My knuckles are covered with the woolen gloves I got from Grandma for Christmas. My breath makes broken patterns on the windshield as I put the car in park. I see nothing of the home through my windows. The door slams shut with a tinny thwack and I step out against the cold. Something crunches under my boot and I kick it over. A square of copper, its corners seafoam green.

All that's left is a cement basement I didn't even know was there, scored between the black-eyed Susans and the bonesets. The air is different. Or is it the way that I am smelling it? Tangled in a thread of frozen grasses I find a frayed line of scarlet and bend down real close to look at it. It waves, mutely, like the thin fins of an eel.

In my pocket sits the weight of an old frame. I pull it into sunlight and stretch out its velvet leg. Set it down on a gray foundation block, grown over pretty with weeds. And then I lie back, on the cold earth, watching the clouds shift their shapes. ◇

Billy

Daphne Carter McKnight

In the pre-dawn dark of a winter weekday
Billy leans in toward the chilly blue bathroom's low-hung mirror
cold white porcelain sink rim pressed against his waist.
Scraping lather and coarse black hairs from his chocolate brown skin
being careful not to wake the family
he talks to his image in a quiet voice
lays out particulars of the day just beginning
calls himself by name as he rinses the shiny silver
double-edged Gillette off under running water.
Steam rising from a hot damp cloth
wrung out in the now-warm basin
fogs the mirror as he wipes stray suds from his chin and ears.
From the open door, light, sound, and scent of Old Spice
spill out into the narrow hallway
drift into the first small bedroom where
his youngest daughter
snuggles deeper under layers of
warm wool blankets and aunt–made quilts
slips softly back into quiet slumber
knowing that she is loved. ◇

The Ladder

Daphne Carter McKnight

and climb
and climb
and climb
and climb
and climb
and climb
and climb
We climb
With cramped blistered hands
On bare calloused feet
With each step upward
Pull the next ones up behind us and
So we mostly hold fast, tighten our grip

Send us all sprawling back down to what?
Threatens to split the ladder in two and
Our collective weight makes the ladder creak and moan
With each step upward

The ladder sways wildly on eroding supports.
The winds of complacency whip us hard
Our destination appears to recede into a farther distance
With each step upward

More treacherous and as slick as glass.
(now spindly and worn from eons of climbers)
Sweat from our palms makes the rungs
The ladder seems to lean a little further backward
With each step upward* ◇

*Thanks to Khaled Mattawa's The Pyramid of Khufu for the line "With each step upward."

The Trial

Rod Carlson

I N 1968, THE PACE OF THE WAR HAD BEEN CRANKED UP AND EVERY-
one in the Air Group at Phu Bai was working overtime. One day,
I'd flown a helicopter north to resupply Marines along the DMZ,
including those on mountain peaks. Repeatedly, we'd hover over a
precipice, with only a tire on a postage-stamp platform, deliver supplies,
and exchange nervous replacements for weary warriors eager to get out
of harm's way and back to the world.

All day, my copilot kept score by logging the number of landings
and the number of times enemy gunners punctured our skin. With
none of us wounded, and the helicopter still in one piece, we kept on
refueling and flying well into the evening until the work was done and
we finally got the green light to head for the barn.

That morning a fellow pilot, Jack Marbury, and I had agreed that
if we beat the odds and survived the day, we'd get a quick shower and
hit the officers' club for dinner, maybe a movie, and several relaxing
drinks. Moderation was my responsibility as Jack had proved himself
to be immoderate in all things. Whenever I sensed he'd had enough to
drink or was otherwise wearing out his welcome, I'd give him the nod
and we'd slog through the mud back to our respective Quonsets. There
we'd pass out and sleep soundly for a few hours until the duty officer
shone a flashlight in our eyes to wake us for the dawn patrol and we'd
begin the routine all over again.

This particular night, by the time I got back to Phu Bai, dinner
was over, the movie was over, and Jack, who was waiting for me in our
squadron's ready room, was indignant that I'd spoiled our evening. He
was ready to hit the sack. Nobody's hitting the sack, I told him, until

I break my fast. The only thing I'd eaten all day was a can of C-ration peaches I gulped down during a fuel stop at noon. Even if it meant eating in the Phu Bai chow hall, I had to eat now. Jack relented and agreed to keep me company.

Crudely built out of rough lumber, plywood, and corrugated steel, the base chow hall had a high ceiling and was as big as a gymnasium or basketball arena. Bad acoustics amplified the constant echo into a painful din. The louder it got, the louder people talked to be heard. Worse than the noise was the stench of industrial cleaning solvents and putrid cooking grease that caused the hardiest of gluttons to skip meals. There were no pictures, no touches of civility, nothing to offset the chow hall's ambiance of total bleakness. But at nearly midnight, the hall was still crowded with returning flight crews and scores of maintenance officers and NCOs who would labor through the night to repair battle damage and ready the aircraft to fly at first light.

In a cordoned-off area, a long table for eight was reserved for the base commander, Colonel Woodley, a non-aviator. He was responsible for the chow hall and everything involving the operation of the base itself. He was not responsible for the Marine Air Group helicopters and crews stationed at the base.

Colonel Woodley was at the table with a brace of well-groomed lieutenant colonels and several majors, all staffers, who wore clean uniforms and bore no resemblance to the rest of us in our filthy green, one-piece flight suits or grungy jungle utilities. At the heavies' table there was an air of sophisticated ebullience. Colonel Woodley was the center of attention and appeared to be presiding over the festivities as if he were the captain of a luxury cruise ship.

Balancing our trays, we walked slowly through the crowded chow hall looking for a place to sit. I spotted a table being vacated and we grabbed it. Jack took a glass of tomato juice off his tray—that's all he was having—and I added our empty trays to a nearby stack. Soon we were joined by two pilots from a Huey gunship squadron. Except for Jack, who sat contemplating his tomato juice, we chewed quickly and talked loudly in clipped sentences hoping to spend no more time there than was absolutely necessary.

Jack had just sprinkled salt and pepper into his tomato juice and was about to give the concoction a stir when suddenly his head snapped to the right. Turning in my chair, I caught a fleeting glimpse of a football-size object on the floor scurrying helter-skelter among the tables en route to the nearest exit. Before I sensed that he'd moved, Jack had covered fifty feet like a nimble terrier. He had the rat in his grip and was down on a knee while his other arm pumped savagely as though wielding a handsaw. While no one had noticed his quarry, no one could miss Jack's exhibition of lightning speed, agility, and manual dexterity. Spontaneous cheers were followed by a brief round of applause, and then sudden silence. Jack had risen from his kneeling position and was smeared with blood up to his elbows. In one hand he held up a bloody spoon and in the other a crimson, headless rat. Then, he dropped the spoon and reached to the floor, picked up something in his fingers, popped it into his mouth, and chewed with an expression of gastronomical ecstasy.

The silence was broken not by more cheers but by groans and muffled retching. I too was aghast. He'd actually eaten the rat's head. It was inconceivable, even for Jack, but I'd seen it and it was dangerously nauseating.

The disgusted murmuring was abruptly squelched by the thunder of heavy feet. It was Colonel Woodley. He'd risen and, like a hulking rhino on stubby legs, was charging toward Jack with his arm outstretched, his finger like the tip of a lance.

Smiling contentedly, as though he'd sunk an impossibly long putt, Jack expected Woodley to offer his hand in congratulations. But he sensed all was not well, and his exuberance vanished.

"You are under arrest!" the colonel bellowed and then turned back to his table and screamed, "Major, get this officer's name and squadron and confine him to quarters." Red-faced and steaming, his eagles gleaming on his collar, Colonel Woodley stormed out the nearest door.

This was my fault. Exhausted and focused on my hunger, I'd failed to notice one critical factor that was now obvious: Jack was half-stewed. When sober, he was somewhat patrician, calculating, quiet, occasionally sarcastic, and frequently remote. But with as little as a bend of the elbow, he'd do a complete Mr. Hyde and become an unpredictable extrovert.

I gave Jack's name and squadron to Woodley's major and promised to get him home and make sure he stayed there.

The next morning, instead of being on the flight schedule, Jack and I were standing tall in front of our squadron's commanding officer, Lieutenant Colonel Adams. An icy veteran of three wars, he'd already expressed his displeasure at Jack and me for bringing disgrace to him and his beloved squadron. I begged his pardon and with all due respect said that all I'd done was to try to eat midnight rations after flying for an ungodly number of hours.

He just scowled and said I'd failed to keep things from going to hell and, as far as he was concerned, I was in as deep shit as Jack. In two days Jack was going to face a summary court martial; worse, I had been appointed Jack's legal counsel. And, he snarled, if we both went down in flames, it was no skin off his ass.

Technically, he added, Jack was entitled to a civilian attorney but with none handy, any officer was legally capable of doing the job. A wry smile formed as he perhaps realized that he was free of the whole mess and he added that a colonel and a court reporter would fly up from Danang to make sure that both the trial and the hanging were kosher.

Although still at attention, I had an overpowering urge to pummel Jack for sucking me into his self-destructive vortex, but out of the corner of my eye, I could see that he was crestfallen. Aw shit, I thought, forget it.

Our C.O. said we had today and tomorrow to prepare. The court would convene the next morning at nine in the base headquarters conference room.

We walked out of the squadron administration office, which was little more than a shack between our ready room and the hangar. Jack fumbled for a smoke. I took the Zippo from his fingers and lit the Camel.

"I guess I finally fucked us both," he said, as though resigned to its inevitability.

But I wasn't listening; suddenly I knew I had a lot of work to do.

Within the hour, I started scouring the base for anything I could find on courts martial. I asked around but our fellow officers were no help. All they could remember was what they'd learned watching "The Caine Mutiny."

I knew that the special court we faced wasn't as bad as a general court that could get you shot at sunrise, but it was still a very serious matter. A summary court could end your career, send you to jail, and make the rest of your life miserable. However, I also remembered that a conviction wasn't automatic. The Uniform Code of Military Justice was created so that any competent officer could step up to the plate, touch all the bases, and be victorious. In addition to the presiding colonel from Danang, the court would consist of two Marine majors and two captains.

As I walked back from the Group Admin office, where I'd borrowed an armful of legal manuals, I was numb with fear but I knew I had to hide it from Jack. I had to keep him feeling positive, but not too positive. I had to keep him away from the O-club bar until the trial was over and he could no longer torpedo our defense.

But there was no defense for what Jack had done. There was no way I could argue that he hadn't done the deed. There were witnesses. Hell, even I was a witness. I told Jack to leave me alone, to stay in his Quonset and rehearse his role of looking like the ideal officer while saying absolutely nothing. Meanwhile, I'd spend the next thirty-six hours reading, memorizing procedures, and filling my brain with legal jargon.

There was one promising note. The prosecuting officer was also a pilot and his tour was almost over. In a few days he'd leave Phu Bai and Vietnam forever. Putting myself in his boots, I knew he had no interest in the trial, no interest in winning or losing; he just wanted out. I hoped he was as confused as I was and that his case was a snarl of loose ends. Maybe he couldn't find convincing witnesses. Maybe he couldn't find precedents on similar cases involving "conduct unbecoming an officer." Such rat-killing cases had to be rare, even in the Marine Corps.

All that was wishful thinking. Even if the prosecution was totally incompetent, we'd still be in trouble. We had no logical defense and, therefore, no case. All I could do was make sure Jack kept a low but dignified profile while I'd keep bobbing and weaving, hoping to avoid a knockout and win the fight on points.

On the morning of the third day, the duty officer woke me, and on my way back from the shower, dressed only in a towel, I stopped to roust Jack. But he was already up, dressed in fresh utilities and looking like a Marine on a recruiting poster. Soon, we'd grabbed some coffee along with enough breakfast to quiet our stomachs, and then, in our most vertical Randolph Scott postures, we arrived at headquarters a few minutes before nine and were ushered into the makeshift courtroom.

The conference table had been turned sideways to accommodate the five stern-faced officers who would determine Jack's fate. We were told to sit on folding chairs facing the court. Several feet to the right, as though there were an official aisle between us, sat the prosecuting officer, Captain Laurence Rabin, who, when cued by the presiding officer, rose and in a monotone read the legal specifications of the crime and then the specific charges, which amounted to the story of that earlier evening's main event, Jack Marbury versus the rat. Then he sat down.

I was shocked. That was his case? No witnesses? No diatribe? No hostile accusations? But the court allowed me no time for confusion. The presiding officer, Colonel Dowd, nodded at me.

I was on. I rose to my full height and took several deep breaths and explained that the prosecutor had failed to prove that Jack's alleged actions met the specifications he'd just read. I then added that Captain Marbury's actions were logical and admirable.

Captain Rabin interrupted and explained that it was an unusual case, to be sure, but considering what had happened, Captain Marbury was certainly guilty if for no other reason than he ate the head of a freshly killed rat.

Colonel Dowd didn't wince or appear squeamish. Looking interested and judicial, he nodded in agreement with the prosecutor.

Not knowing if I was about to violate legal protocol, I continued. "Gentlemen, it seems that if we're going to speak of behavior we should understand a little of the character of the defendant. Captain Jack Marbury is a highly decorated and qualified Marine aviator whose actions, often spontaneous and reflexive, have saved countless lives and delivered many Marines from grave danger. Secondly, it is important that the court consider another factor relative to the chow hall itself. A facility dedicated to preparing and serving food to United States Marines is no place for any type of vermin, especially a disgusting, disease-ridden Vietnamese rat. It is hardly a stretch to say that the presence of such a creature constitutes a threat to our Marines and therefore is a threat to our national security. By acting instantly and eliminating the rat, Captain Marbury exhibited great presence of mind and should be commended for his dedication to duty. Although I'm loath to cast aspersions, it is obvious that the base commander's reaction was more irrational and excessive than Captain Marbury's, no doubt because he has no current experience with the blood and gore of combat that Captain Marbury faces on a daily basis."

Then Captain Rabin, feeling obligated to get back in the fray, objected. "What about Captain Marbury eating the head of the rat? That's hardly acceptable behavior for an officer and a gentleman."

"I agree, hardly acceptable behavior, indeed. . . ." But before I could add the proverbial punch line *that with no evidence there was no case,* Jack was on his feet.

"Gentlemen," he said, "I must set the record straight. I was merely following my instinct when I killed that rat, and when I realized what I'd done, naturally I was embarrassed and so to make a joke out of the whole miserable business, I pretended to eat . . . . "

Colonel Dowd broke in. "You're telling the court *you palmed it?*"

"Precisely," Jack said. "Colonel, I have never on that or any occasion eaten the head of a rat or any other rodent."

As I motioned him back to his chair, I felt a heart-stopping chill. We're done for. Regardless of the legal technicalities and Rabin's failings as a prosecutor, they'd never buy Jack's yarn.

Colonel Dowd looked to his left, then right, to gauge the reaction of the other officers. None appeared to have any questions, but a few crooked lips suggested the court was struggling to suppress its response.

Dowd then addressed me and Jack and Captain Rabin. "Gentlemen, step outside while the court deliberates."

We took several steps down the hall to avoid the appearance of eavesdropping and stopped.

"God, I'll be glad when this mess is over," Rabin said, but before I could agree with him, a thunderous clap of laughter echoed from the conference room and then the door opened and we were waved back inside.

With considerable trepidation, we walked soberly to our chairs and stood at attention.

"Captain Marbury, this court finds you not guilty. You're dismissed."

My first instinct was to whoop in celebration, and then I wanted to punch Jack in the nose for dragging me through this ordeal, but I refrained. The three of us, spontaneously and in unison, executed right faces and marched out the door. It was over. Jack was free.

But I was still baffled. Had my speech won the day? Or was it Jack's testimony? I didn't believe his story, but now I wasn't sure what I'd seen him do. I was sure, however, that the First Marine Air Wing had no desire to convict Jack or to let a non-aviator like Woodley sandbag one of its pilots.

We walked outside. Marines on a sanitation detail had just ignited kerosene and were burning human waste in a drum next to a latrine. A puff of wind swirled a dervish of black smoke around us. Despite the reek of burning sewage, taking deep breaths and silently savoring our victory was pure euphoria. Then, with the hope of getting back on the flight schedule for the afternoon launch, we started walking toward the sound of helicopter engines and our squadron ready room.

I could tell Jack had been stewing and wanted to say something, perhaps to apologize for dragging me through hell.

Suddenly he stopped and glared. "I'm shocked. You actually thought I ate it, didn't you?"

"Nothing you did would surprise me," I said.

When we got to the ready room, Jack opened the screen door for me. "Would it surprise you if I told you how grateful I am for your friendship?"

"Yeah, that really would surprise me," I said.

He laughed and we went inside to check out the mission board. ◇

Gebre Wins the Marathon (NYC)

James K. Zimmerman

he dreams of time dripping down in cool
mountain rain and blue-green rivers as he runs

a hunger his people a hunger without end

in his mind's eye a forest of people brown
as coffee strong as the Lion of Judah and
beautiful as his ancient hills of Zion

and a thirst knowing no end in water poured
over head and down throat and through
the words of his father and his father's father

and he runs with the people for his people
his body flowing like the blue-green river
in the mountains and he sees timeless dreams
in canyons of concrete and steel and glass
and he knows the mountain rain in his stride
his hunger his hope

and still a deepening thirst that does not stop
with the cheering and the faces and the dream
and the tape at the finish line

a hunger his people a hunger without end ◇

Shond Khay

Loretta Oleck

grandma called her Jewish Shanghai
ghetto on the banks of the Huangpu River

shond khay, shame of life—

ten strangers in one room

some prayed some slept some planned some wept

grandma slithered away to shed her skin

hard and calloused ghetto walls rolled
off her bones shattering into a trail
of petrified stones

she cautiously tiptoed over them
like walking a tight rope

believing in guides
guised as spirits and ghosts

harboring deep faith in what could
never be proved or seen

grandma lived in a shell
of a self-constructed dream
where with bare hands she dug up the earth—
an archeologist collecting specimens
of yesterday's worth—

a shrunken mushroom a leathery pebble pod
a wispy fern a hornet's nest

these became treasures in her new American world—
measures of what once was and what could be her future

treasures that weighed her down overflowing
from her deep cardigan pockets

she waited at the hem of the woods
waited until dawn tugged at her brow
to break into a hopeful jigsaw dance—

side-slap shimmy-step barefoot
kicking up star moss and blue stone
sun spinning zydeco—

what a far cry from the Jewish Shanghai ghetto

what a far cry from

shond khay ◇

Jive

Clark Cooke

TAKE A SEAT AND A SIP, DEAR READER. LET ME BRING YOU UP TO speed.

Here I am, a Self-Portrait: Nappy hair, face mottled with pimples; fingertips stained yellow from tobacco, fingernails half-chewed, jagged-edged; three days' worth of caked sweat in between my legs, under my arms, on my balls.

And here's a Family Photo, Fragmented: My Parents: Yes, they'd made it. Pulled themselves up from the Bottom of the Well, scaled the Bell Curve, bridged the Achievement Gap, and slipped onto the Affirmative Action Express, chooo choooo!

They rode the express north out of Brooklyn, got off in Larchmont, N.Y., where I was raised. Where I was the only black kid in the fourth-grade class. So the teacher sent me packing, sent my thick-rimmed glasses and seven-inch afro out the door and down the hall. Down to where the other two black kids in the school, alongside a poor white boy and a stuttering Mexican, huddled over remedial texts. The other two black kids in the school, who snickered and called me nigger when I passed them on the playground. Four days of testing. Math, reading comprehension, logic. Four days until the special ed teacher realized that I didn't belong in that classroom. Four days until I walked back down the hallway, handed a note to my bemused fourth-grade teacher, and reclaimed my seat by the window.

But I eventually made it out of fourth grade. Fifth, sixth, seventh, eighth, then high school.

75

Mamaroneck. Tenth grade, French class. Sitting in the back row, slumping in the chair, hoping Miss Gueuledecon wouldn't call on me. But she always did. And I'd stammer a response. Horrible pronunciation. And a few of the ass-kissing students in the front row would giggle, cover their mouths, try to muffle their laughter. And I'd wonder why I hadn't taken Spanish and why we had to study these stupid foreign languages. That we would never use anyway. But sometimes I didn't make it to class and didn't have to suffer *that* particular humiliation. But there was always another one waiting around the corner or in the North Hall lounge where the black and Puerto Rican kids hung out. Where they waited for my glasses and oversized backpack and disheveled hair to pass by so they could laugh and point. Laughing and pointing on the days when they didn't feel like chasing me through hallways, backpack jostling, straps digging into my shoulders, my skinny arms pumping, wobbly legs churning, and behind me *Get 'im Get 'im,* behind me twisted, contorted, laughing, cackling faces, *WHERE YOU GOIN'?* And they chase me and chase me until SPLAT. I crash into something. A wall, other students, the floor. And behind me the laughter exploding. And me, on my hands and knees, scrambling for my glasses and the books and papers that had spilled out of my backpack. And the bell for next period rings and the laughter dies down, disappears, and the mob heads back to the other side of school.

The other side of the tracks, past the bridge. That's where most of those kids came from. The other side of town. No gangs, crackheads, or cowboy bebopping coppers. No urban black and brown American clichés. Not really. Train tracks, auto body shops, Central American immigrants, stench of gasoline heavy in the air. A few low-key patrol cars, a garbage truck garage. A little stretch of land where most of the black and brown kids hailed from, called the Flats. Flat land of the town, part of the town that flooded every spring. Garages, basements, first floors, everything sucked and swallowed by the rising water. A few Italian families still around. Some black ones too. As well as drunks with mismatched shoes and socks. Homeless dudes scratching their dirty black-and-gray beards, pushing shopping carts filled with bottles. Stopping at trashcans, reaching, digging, searching, scrounging,

Dumpster-diving for cans, bottles, leftovers, and whatever they could get their fingers on.

And I scooped up my glasses, stuffed the loose papers and books back into my backpack. The bell stopped ringing. If I hurried I could still make it to class. But I didn't feel like hurrying or sitting in class. So I left school and wandered up Boston Post Road, no destination in mind, but I always ended up at the same place. I tried to walk past, but the smell of grease and French fries and burning meat sucked me in, sucked me under the golden arches. McDonald's.

Alone in a booth in the back. And I'd stare around with sad eyes, feel sorry for myself. Stuffing my face, wolfing down fries, orange sodas, and twenty-piece Chicken McNuggets. All three sauces. Barbecue, Sweet 'n Sour, and Honey Mustard. I'd dip six nuggets in each. Then the last two in whichever were left. Then I'd belch, burp, rub my belly, and once the food settled, and the belching and burping ended, I went back to school. Trudged back down the Boston Post Road.

COLLEGE WAS THE WAY OUT. Out of monochromatic Larchmont. And Howard University, the Mecca of black gals with mocha skin and Jack and Jill memberships, was my first choice.

"No child of mine is going to any all-black school," my father answered. And then my sister, all braces and barrettes, "Mom, what's an all-black school?"

I ended up across town from the smell of Ben's Chili Bowl and the break beats of D.C. go-go, in the middle of the white triangle on the campus of George Washington University.

I spent the first two years rollicking in rickety dorm beds with Laura, Lisa, Janet, Nina (the bronzed Israeli chick), and Deborah with the tongue ring. Because at overpriced, private universities it wasn't just the fat chicks who dated black, the ones who smuggled extra muffins out of the cafeteria. Nope. It was possible to get a white girl like Laura or Lisa or Nina or Deborah.

But I didn't last too long at George Washington. Too much pot and red wine. Too many late nights and skipped classes. Too many afternoons spent in the park, on a bench. Reading.

In a park, on a bench. A few feet away from a pond. Quack, quack. A clutch of ducks, necks bent, beaks stabbing at the ground. A woman's stooped back. Her wrinkled, red-spotted hand scattered breadcrumbs. And I'm on a bench, book on my lap, pen in hand. In my pocket, a bag of tobacco, rolling papers, and a lighter. Reading, eyes scanning the page, connecting the dots. Missing another class, blowing off another homework assignment, reading Cecil Brown's *The Life and Loves of Mr. Jiveass Nigger*.

FFFFFFFFFF. Ten consecutive classes, failed. Teetering on the brink of expulsion, knee-deep in academic probation. Two straight semesters pissed and smoked and shitted away. Both times I'd registered for classes, bought the books, and promised myself that I would go. This semester it'll be different. I'll wake up for that ten o'clock class, get ahead on the reading, start my papers a week in advance, and attend the professor's office hours.

And I did. And everything went well, for the first month. Then one day, I wouldn't make it to class. No big deal, it was just one. But the next day, I'd run into someone on campus, head back to their apartment, and smoke. A joint, a blunt, a bong hit, whatever. And just like that I'd miss another class, maybe two. Then I'd panic and realize that I had a paper or a project due in two days. And then, not worrying about the consequences, I'd say fuck it. Fuck homework, fuck classes, fuck school.

And a couple of weeks later I was back to my regular schedule. Late-night naps, waking up mid-afternoon. Jittery fingers, dry mouth, lips sticking together. Breakfast of black coffee and cigarettes. And I'd tramp to the park. Stay there reading, smoking, scribbling in the margins, mumbling to myself.

And it was all that extracurricular reading that got me kicked out of school, landed me back in Larchmont. Back in my parents' basement. Yep, I was one of those boomerang kids, *Slouching Toward Adulthood* and all that. Another failed, feckless millennial. With a thirty-thousand-pound student-loan ball and chain around my ankles. And the only way to get it off was to go to work. So I hopped on the New Haven line and headed south.

I GOT OFF THE TRAIN at 125th Street. Dragged my legs through Harlem's bleary, early-morning streets. Covered my nose as I walked past a pile of garbage, recoiled from a homeless dude who jumped around, mumbling to himself, no shirt on his charcoal chest. I was desperate for another cup of coffee, a few cigarettes, five more hours of sleep. Three weeks on the job and I still hadn't gotten used to this routine.

The job involved Sheetrocking, painting, and plugging up holes. A thick-necked Jamaican guy had guided me through the first few weeks. He'd shown me the ropes, taught me what I had to know, and bragged about all the pussy he used to get back home. Kingston, capital city. The strip clubs, every day after work. But now he was gone. Off in Brooklyn or the Bronx. Tiling floors, painting empty apartments, driving tenants out of buildings. Whatever the landlord asked.

Frederick Douglass Boulevard and 145th Street. In front of the building. Dealers with do-rags and red eyes, waiting for their first customers, watching solo moms rush their kids off to school. Peeping the scene with stoned faces, purple haze blurring their vision. Watching taxis, trucks, buses rushing down Harlem's gentrified arteries. I nodded at them. They returned the greeting. Best to stay out of each other's way. They had a job to do and so did I. I trudged past them, tool bag in hand, walked through two double doors, then slowly climbed up one, then two, then three flights. Brown paint chipping off the wall, a layer of dust on the marble steps, smell of turkey bacon beating back the stale piss. And from up above, two, three flights up above, I heard the clop-clop of a suitcase banging against the steps. It banged on every step. The sound got closer and closer. A brown-skin lady lumbered down the steps. Two plaid suitcases in her hands, two beige children tugging at her arms. Today's lucky losers, I assumed. The tenants that hadn't paid tried to sneak back in and were getting kicked out again. They looked the part. The tired, haggard, beat-down faces. Sometimes people crept up the fire escape, slipped in through an open window. Other times they busted the lock off the door.

I moved up against the wall to let them pass. I kept my mouth shut. Nothing to say. Sorry, I hate to have to do this. Would have been stupid. You'll find somewhere else to live. Yeah, there were a lot of empty shelters and street corners. I stared into the woman's eyes, yellow and puffy. She straightened her back, brushed a tangle of synthetic hair from her face, smiled at me, then said good morning. No irony or bitterness or anger. My lips were stuck together, throat clenched. I hadn't expected her to say anything, hadn't expected her to smile. Maybe she was so beat down, so resigned to her fate that she didn't have the strength or energy to be angry. I passed them on the steps, turned around. The suitcase clop-clopping on each step. One of the kids turned, wiped snot from his nose, and waved at me. It gave me chills. I shivered. Fuck. This whole thing seemed so fucked up. I couldn't smile or wave back. I sucked in the smell of turkey bacon and stale piss. I felt like throwing up. It wasn't even nine o'clock yet. I went up two more flights, threw my bag down, and waited.

The front door of the building creaked open and a voice boomed through the stairwell. The landlord, my boss. He made his way up the steps. Three floors away, but I could already hear him huffing and grunting. Could see his brown cheeks billowing, sweat dripping down his fat neck, sliding under his collar, staining his button-down shirt. His chest heaved. He wiped his neck with a paper napkin, leaned against the wall. "She try to come back?"

"Who?" I asked.

"The pregnant girl. You didn't see her?"

I shook my head. "I don't think so," I said. I told him about the woman with the two kids.

"No, that's Mrs. Monroe. One of the good ones. Here," he said, and handed me a lock. Thick steel. "This should keep them out." Cold, thick steel in my palm. "It was a young girl. And her boyfriend." He snickered. "One of the kids dealing drugs outside."

His phone rang. He pulled it out of his chest pocket, then turned his back to me. Huge sweat stains on the back of his shirt. He walked down a few steps, turned back around and pointed at the door in front of me. He covered the phone and said, "Go in. Make sure there's nobody in there. Then lock'er up."

I reached into my tool bag, grabbed the metal head of a hammer just in case someone was still inside the apartment. I slid my fingers down to the rubber handle, squeezed. My body, tense. Legs, a bit wobbly. Twelve bucks an hour. Hauling buckets of paint and plaster, unloading big-ass pieces of Sheetrock, and plugging up leaky ceilings. Now I had to chase drug dealers and their pregnant girlfriends out of locked-up apartments. Shit. Waking up and going to class didn't seem so bad anymore. Wish I could have worked this job years ago. I would have never cut another class.

I pushed the door, jumped back. The lights were off. Sunlight was coming in through one of the windows. Smell of cooked food, blunt smoke, old clothes. Most of the apartment empty. A table stacked with bottles, aluminum and plastic. And in a corner a big black garbage bag. Maybe it was their stash. Drugs and guns left behind in the scramble to get out of the apartment. Out the window, down the fire escape, and into the street. I peered into the bag, sifted through it. Old clothes, baby clothes. And underneath the clothes, CDs and DVDs. No stash. I heard sounds, street sounds. I gripped the hammer. They were coming from the bedroom, through an open window. Inside the bedroom, covers torn off the bed, lying in a heap on the floor. Scarface poster on the wall. Basketball sneakers neatly lined up against the wall. I heard more street sounds. The window was half open. It led out onto a fire escape. Six stories off the ground. On the windowsill, an empty baggy. Probably a dime sack. I looked down for more. Nothing. I got down on my hands and knees, peered under the bed. Holy shit. I extended my arm, grabbed a plastic bag. A quart-sized Ziploc, stuffed with baggies like the one on the sill. But they weren't empty. They were filled with weed, packed tight with twenty-sacks. The weed, purple. I opened the bag, pulled out one of the baggies, opened it, let my nose suck up the smell. Damn good shit. Purple haze. Fresh, just off the boat. They'd definitely be coming back for this.

I spread the baggies on the bed, started counting. Ten, fifteen, twenty, twenty-five.

"Clark!" A voice from the hallway. I froze. Then panicked. Oh, shit. I gathered up the baggies, jammed them by the fistful back into the bag.

"You find anything?" The door creaking open. "Where are you?"

"Back here," I yelled, then scooped up the last of the baggies. I heard his feet stomping through the apartment.

He poked his head into the bedroom. "Find anything? What are these clothes?" On the floor, a couple of piles of adult clothes. He walked over to the window, slammed it down. "Need to put some guards on these damn windows. That your hammer?" I'd left it on the windowsill. I picked it up and followed him out of the apartment.

Back in the hallway. Loud feet coming down the steps, and the sound of a black garbage bag being dragged. Willie, the super, fat and chocolaty black, plodded down the steps, black garbage bag in hand, work gloves on, three gold chains around his neck.

"Nasty motherfucka," he said.

"What happened?" I asked, smiling at him. I knew it must have been pretty bad.

"This nigga up in 9A, Murray, diabetic motherfucka. Let his toilet overflow for three fucking days and his cats shitting everywhere on the floor." He kicked the garbage bag. It seemed full.

The landlord looked Willie up and down, shook his head, then turned to me. "You see anything funny in there? Drugs, guns, money?"

I swallowed hard, then said no.

He sighed. "I'm so sick of these damn people."

These damn people who looked just like he did, like all three of us. Same Brillo-pad hair, bulbous noses, high melanin count. I averted my eyes, hung my head, nodded. When I looked up Willie was smiling at me. "Good luck, he said. "With that bathroom in 8A."

I didn't know what he was talking about.

"Yeah," the landlord said. "Get all that crap cleaned up and patch up the ceiling. Just enough to hold till Monday. Take these." He handed me a fresh pair of work gloves. Then headed down the steps. But quickly turned back around. "You *sure* you didn't see anything in there?"

I shook my head, jammed a hand into my pocket. My fingers brushed against the Ziploc bag. I cleared my throat and said no.

"Alright, good. Last thing I need is them trying to get back in there."

Five, six, seven hundred dollars of weed in my pocket. Options, I had plenty. But I wasn't sure what to do. Smoke some, then find people in Mamaroneck who'd buy the rest. I could pocket some good money, find one or two people to buy in bulk, or I could sell all of it and really make some money. Or I could smoke it all. Two months since I'd smoked and it seemed like a year. I was starting to miss it, starting to get bored with sobriety.

I heard the front doors of the building creaking open, voices coming up the stairwell. *C'mon nigga. How you know? I know. C'mon.* Boots stomping up the steps. I grabbed my bag, tiptoed up the two flights, gently knocked on the door.

8A Hernandez. Fragmented Sheetrock surrounded the toilet. I had to pick up the pieces, patch up the hole. I slipped on the cotton canvas gloves, scooped up the pieces of piss- and shit-logged Sheetrock, held my breath, watched maggots scurry and dive in and out of the crevices, in between my fingers. Behind me I heard, "Mira, mira." Hernandez, with sunken cheeks and scarlet eyes, was pointing up to the ceiling. "The guy arriba ... moreno ... crazy!"

I nodded, told him to back up, so I could do my work. I measured the hole, cut a piece of Sheetrock. Placed it over the hole, nailed it into the wood beams. Then spread plaster into the cracks, and slowly smoothed tape down over those same cracks. Put another layer of plaster over the tape. And told him it was finished.

"It no look good," he said.

It did look like shit. I hadn't smoothed down the tape enough and it was already starting to lose its grip. And I probably hadn't mixed the plaster and cement right. Fuck it. "Don't worry," I said, then picked up my hammer and screw gun. "It'll hold till Monday."

JOB DONE. Day over. Time to catch the train at 125th Street. But I still hadn't decided what to do about the baggies. All that weed. It must have belonged to the kids who hustled in front of the building. And they probably knew that I'd put the new lock on the apartment. And in their weed-induced paranoia, they'd probably suspect that I'd uncovered their stash. What to do? I could walk by them, pretend I didn't know anything, ignore their searching, questioning stares, duck my head and walk away, take a zigzag route to the train station. But what if they rushed me, waited for me to turn a corner, then grabbed my shoulders, threw me into a wall. No, I couldn't get away with that. Not in this neighborhood. But fuck, I needed that money. And they could always get more pot.

I walked down the stairs slowly, still trying to figure out what to do. Hopefully, those kids, the ones with the burnt-out eyes, scratchy voices, and sagging jeans, wouldn't be there. They should have been in school, high school. But instead they had set up shop on the front steps. On fucking Frederick Douglass Boulevard. But if they weren't there everything would be fine. Maybe the cops had spooked them, walked down the block shoulder-to-shoulder in a show of force. Or maybe a few patrol cars had parked across the street. If they weren't there it'd be easy. I would just walk out the front door, make my zigzag turns, and I'd be gone. No reason to worry about being jumped, thrown against a wall, or threatened.

I got down to the ground level, slowly approached the double doors. And through the graffiti-stained Plexiglas I saw them. A pack, a huddle. I went through the first double door. And all heads, maybe five of them, turned toward me. My hand on the door handle. Their eyes peering through the stained glass. I stopped, waited, nodded, nodded again. Some talking amongst them. Then one of them walked toward me, toward the door, up the front steps. He looked left, then right, quickly pulled the door open. Baby face, no pimples or blemishes, pointy goatee on his chin. No words, just eyes. I pulled the plastic bag out of my pocket, extended my hand. He stared at it, then up at me. Surprise, fear, apprehension in his eyes. I wasn't sure which. I felt his fingernails scrape through my palm. And the bag was gone. He stuffed it into his pants, nodded, turned his back to me, and went through the second set of doors. Before going out, I waited. Not long, just a few minutes, then I pushed the door open. All the heads turned toward me. I couldn't see the eyes under the low-brimmed baseball caps. No words, just head nods. And I hurried down the block.

I walked through the Harlem crowds. 125th Street. All shades of black people. Brown, beige, and yellow. The people I'd grown up so far away from. And here I was among them. Smelling like them, body aching like them. Jeans splattered with paint, boots stained with shit. Plaster and piss. And I felt strong, looked healthy. I wasn't the nerdy black kid with clusters of pimples, an afro, and scraggly arms. Faded skin, the color of second-hand book pages. That was me no more. The sun had darkened my skin. Six weeks of carrying buckets of paint and plaster had sculpted my arms, broadened my shoulders. Protein-packed meals had bulked my chest.

And the way the women stared, no, ogled at me. Black women, brown women. Their eyes roving up and down, pausing to check out the package, the bulge in my tight jeans, tight jeans hugging my ass. My cock jumping, each time one of those pretty Puerto Rican girls flashed me a smile. More blood pumping through it, more sensitive than ever. Weeks, no, months, since I'd jerked off.

My old bohemian self had fallen away. That bullshit role I'd written for myself. Malnourished, decadent, fin de siècle, cigarette-smoking, dreaming of pink nipples and pale flesh. Jamming my head between quivering thighs. My body too weak to fuck. Legs too weak to thrust.

And the way the other men, black and brown men, stared at me. The men who swayed from side to side when they walked, who mumbled rap lyrics under their breath, who would turn and spin and gawk at every passing thick ass. The way they stared at me. Their eyes. Insecure, aggressive, hostile. As if we were battling for territory. Me, the nerd with the burnt-out lungs and jittery fingers. But the boots, the jeans, and the broad shoulders changed everything. They were my disguise. Even with the glasses, I was still imposing. As if they could sense I was stronger and healthier than they were, could see the bulge in my pants, and the veins running through my cock.

They stared. They noticed me.

But on the train things were different. I was just another worker, not worth staring at. Just another dirty, paint-stained, shit-smelling worker. Plaster and dirt under my fingernails.

ON THE TRAIN RIDING HOME. The high of walking through those Harlem crowds, the satisfaction of those stares, gone. Now my body felt sore. Everything ached. I wanted to sit down, stretch, shut my eyes, but I couldn't. This was rush hour. Metro-North. And it was packed. Business crowd, suits and blouses, ties and BlackBerrys. Express train, with stops in New Rochelle, Larchmont, Mamaroneck, and Harrison. Wall Street folk. Bankers, brokers, hedge-fund managers. The fathers and mothers of the people I'd grown up with. My peers. The ones who had made something of themselves or were poised to. And here I was splattered with the same shit as the other day laborers. The early worm who toiled in the mud all day. And there they were. But all that otherness. That funky-ass French cheese, the country-club membership. All that didn't mean shit now. I was just another worker. And there they were, barely making eye contact with me. Their heads buried behind newspapers. *Financial Times, Wall Street Journal, New York Times.*

These doughy fathers and soccer moms who'd invited me for sleepovers, driven me to Little League games, hugged me at graduation. Now they ignored me, couldn't recognize me. Or they frowned or flashed an awkward tight-lipped, disconcerted smile. So I stood in the vestibule, leaned my head back, and closed my eyes. I didn't feel like asking them if I could sit down. Asking them to move their briefcases or jackets or sandwiches off the seat. I was just another black. Member of the permanent underclass. Dirty, with broad shoulders and a scruffy neck. Returning to my parents' basement in Larchmont. A/C-regulated home, fully stocked fridge, recently mopped floors. I smiled. They couldn't recognize me. Not the people on the train, or the people in Harlem, or the grimy workers thronged around me. I leaned back, closed my eyes, and the train rumbled on. ◇

Night Poem

Carla Carlson

Nighttime, and I am alone, naked
in down, protected by my small light,
the solace of turning pages.
I can't bear to see beyond my safe shroud
to your unwrecked side. You are not here
to bother me or make me giggle.
You are not here and that is all.
It will take an epic story, a giant pill.
Where are you my lullaby?
The chair is not a chair.
The air is cold. ◇

Departing

Malea Baer

Stitch my ear to your heart that I may hear it go—
Stomp barefoot in the garden at midnight
Scream hymns at noon that I may hear.

When your heart no longer goes—
when your feet no longer beat the earth,
and your voice has been extinguished,

I will dress you,
drape your mirrors and windows,
bind my mouth.

All I ask—
    wait for me ◇

Three Perceptions of Auschwitz

Hubert Babinski

I VISITED THE AUSCHWITZ CONCENTRATION CAMP FOR THE FIRST TIME in May 1965, when I was a young graduate student intent on exploring my family's Polish background and on discovering my own connection to my Polish roots. I revisited the camp two more times, in 1998 and 2010, when I was much older, better informed, and less idealistic. Auschwitz, too, was different each time, revealing to me how a place where inhuman events happened could change in presentation and perception over a long period of time.

In 1947 a distant relative of my father sponsored her Polish cousin to come to the United States, as so many Polish-Americans did with relatives in those days. This cousin, who had escaped occupied Poland early in the war as a young man, had become attached to the American army that liberated Belsen and Dachau. He showed me and my family photographs he had taken of emaciated people in barrack-like buildings, jammed onto three levels of what looked like giant bunk beds, all hollow-eyed and staring blankly at the photographer. Outside those buildings were heaps of dead bodies, really skin-and-bones skeletons, people who died of hunger and disease and were to be bulldozed into mass graves. His pictures and stories of such human brutality terrified me, though I pretended they didn't. I was eleven.

YEARS LATER, IN 1965, I was studying at the Polish Institute of Literary Research in Warsaw, and working on an article for a literary journal in Kraków. At that time, I thought of Auschwitz as a concentration camp, a general term for the Nazi camps that I had learned in the United States. But Auschwitz, originally Polish army barracks, had been turned into a slave labor camp by the Nazis, its prisoners working either within the camp or in factories or as menial laborers outside the camp. Its range of killing methods included a gas chamber and crematorium, but its capacity for mass murder was limited. By contrast, Birkenau was designed as an extermination camp, where Jews, Gypsies, homosexuals, and others deemed undesirable by the Nazis were gassed and cremated. These distinctions among camps were not clear to me on that first visit, and I did not see Birkenau until 1998.

During my stay in Kraków, Jan Goślicki, my official mentor from the Institute, and the young poet Michał Sprusiński, whose father had died in Auschwitz as the result of medical experiments, suggested I read Tadeusz Borowski's *Farewell to Maria* (1948; reissued in 1964), a book of short stories about his experiences in Auschwitz from 1943 to 1944. (The English title is *This Way to the Gas Chamber, Ladies and Gentlemen.*) They said I would learn more by reading Borowski than by going to the camp, which was perhaps their desire to shield me from actually seeing the camp but also to distance themselves from that awful time in their lives. *Farewell to Maria* and Borowski's earlier collection, *We Were in Auschwitz* (1946), are still among the most powerful and frightening evocations of life in that camp. Books could not replace my walking on those grounds and in those buildings where so many had suffered and died. But they would, however, help me to grasp more acutely what I would see and to understand what had been inflicted upon and endured by the prisoners in that deadly place.

I was having coffee one afternoon in the Hotel Francuski café in Kraków with Jan Goślicki when he pointed out a man sitting at a nearby table. He told me that the man had been a Kapo in Auschwitz and was now a prominent member of the Polish Communist Party. Kapos were often criminals with police records or just men who thrived on cruelty. They ran teams of prisoners as work gangs and had the power of life and death over their charges. In exchange for colluding with Nazis, Kapos were given special privileges like decent food and shelter. For Jan the Kapo-Communist Party connection was natural: yet another example of the "crooks running the country," as Jan liked to say. "How could such an evil man rise to such political prominence?" I asked. Jan lit yet another cigarette, inhaled deeply, and blew a few smoke rings before declaiming: "Communism is just another form of Nazism. It's all totalitarianism, Hugh, it's the Polish Mafia." I was not naive about corruption in high places, but I was more an idealist then and believed—or wanted to believe—that virtue was rewarded and evil punished more often than not. This Kapo's life seemed such a repudiation of basic human values, his political prominence a travesty. I was shocked and appalled. Jan drank his beer and crushed his cigarette butt on his plate. "Hugh," he said, "you have a lot to learn about the People's Republic of Poland, our leaders, and how this society and the government really work. Make this your first lesson." I knew he was right about Poland but also about my Catholic sense of human nature and how people use and abuse power. That afternoon was an awakening to a more sophisticated political sense and another spur for me to see Auschwitz.

After my conversations about Auschwitz with Jan and Michał, I made a special effort to see Andrzej Munk's unfinished film *Pasażerka*, "The Passenger." This powerful film, available on DVD today, is about the women workers in Auschwitz-Birkenau who sorted the belongings of the thousands arriving by train transport, most of whom were sent almost immediately to the showers/Zyklon B gas chambers, and about the female Nazi guards who taunted and mistreated the women workers. In 1942, part of Auschwitz had been fenced off and reserved for women. Seeing the film provided even further motivation for me to visit the camp, but also its brutal treatment of people, incarceration methods, and ethnic cleansing (to use a modern term) gave me some insight into Jan's claim that Fascism and Stalinist Communism were bedfellows.

On my first visit to Auschwitz I went alone because my Kraków colleagues and friends knew only too well what had happened there, having been taken on school trips as children. In some cases members of their families had died or barely survived their imprisonment, and these friends avoided further reminders of those horrors.

On a sunny morning in May 1965, I boarded the train in Kraków for the forty-kilometer ride to Oświęcim. I was the only person to get off the train there, and the stationmaster pointed me toward a road leading into the countryside. I came upon simple brick and wooden houses, barnyards with chickens and geese, fields of rye already tall and flowering potato plants. The ordinariness surprised me. When I arrived at the camp I realized that anyone living in the vicinity must have known what was happening at the end of that road. The camp was so obvious and, pleading ignorance, as I knew so many people living in the vicinity had, seemed glaringly false. The Nazis had evacuated the farms and houses immediately surrounding Auschwitz-Birkenau, but many farmers and workers living just outside that perimeter had to have known. Many years later, when I saw the film *Shoah*, the interviews with the people living in the neighborhood and the cheerful railroad engineer describing the arriving trainloads of prisoners only strengthened my sense that anyone living in the vicinity knew but chose to deny the facts, perhaps for their own safety and their families' lives, or perhaps—more forgivably—because denial of the atrocities preserved one's sanity. The smoke and the odor of burning flesh from the ovens would have been unmistakable. What must it have been like to smell that everyday?

A beautiful linden tree stood near the *Arbeit Macht Frei* (Work Makes You Free) sign over the Auschwitz gate, and off to the left was a small kiosk that sold postcards and booklets about the camp. I was struck by the realization that, with the exception of the kiosk, the physical surroundings were very close to what prisoners saw when they entered the camp. I walked through Auschwitz alone—row upon row of red brick buildings surrounded by two barbwire fences three meters apart. The walls lining the corridors of some prisoners' barracks had photographs that had been preserved in the German files, with the inmates' prison numbers sewn on the uniforms and also burned on their arms, others with a last name printed on their photographs, and still others with no identification at all. Here and there, a carnation or a rose had been left on the picture frame of a deceased prisoner. Each corridor wall held hundreds of photographs. It was haunting to see those head shots of men and women in their classic striped prison uniforms, looking straight ahead, all with slightly bulging eyes, glassy from hunger and overwork, staring at another inmate's photograph staring back across the corridor—a macabre gallery. The Nazi rage for order produced catalogues of photos.

In Block 11, the Death Block, people were forced to stand jammed up against one another in tiny unvented cells to die of starvation and suffocation. In the courtyard of the building several posts were planted in the ground where 20,000 prisoners had been tied and shot by firing squads. The doorway to that courtyard had a stone doorsill worn down by the feet of the thousands of people who crossed it only to be shot moments later. I could imagine the shuffle of those feet, the voices that screamed in fear, anger, or defiance, the last desperate whispers of friends. Death was palpable in that courtyard, and I felt surrounded by ghosts.

The huge bins of human hair; children's shoes; stacks of suitcases with people's names, cities, and towns written or scrawled in chalk across them; the heaps of eye glasses; and the piles of tin plates, knives, and forks on display behind smudged Plexiglas walls horrified me. I was the lone visitor in the camp buildings that afternoon, and as I moved from horror to horror, I tried to imagine what it might have felt like to be a prisoner here. Borowski's stories and Munk's film came back to me full force as did the photographs of the camps I had seen as a child.

I walked around outside the buildings, looking through the barb-wire fences and gazing up at the sentry towers. I had heard that those who could no longer bear life in Auschwitz sometimes threw themselves against those wires to electrocute themselves. Looking around that prison yard, at the machinery of death that had been so carefully designed as though it were some harmless manufacturing process, I reflected on the diabolical nature of the Nazi mind and the terror under which the inmates lived. I was not sure whether I would have been able to endure life under such viciousness. I, too, might have sought the solace of those electric wires.

I walked back to the station and took the next train to Kraków. None of my Kraków friends asked me about my visit and, taking this cue about their reluctance, I volunteered nothing.

MY SECOND VISIT OCCURRED during the summer of 1998, when my wife and I went to Kraków to meet some Polish and English friends. I had arranged with my English friends—the husband an avid historian who knew more about wartime Kraków than I—that we would go to Auschwitz together. I told them about my first visit, in 1965, and said I would be glad to be their guide. I wondered how I would feel during another visit, considering I had more than 30 years of additional knowledge about wartime Poland and Auschwitz.

From the Hotel Francuski, where my wife and I were staying for old time's sake, my friend and I hired a driver who got us to Auschwitz in about an hour. He parked in a large lot filled with cars and buses that had not been there in 1965. Across from the lot a large auditorium showed a documentary film about Auschwitz-Birkenau every half hour; a large store sold books, posters, and camp "souvenirs"; and a restaurant served refreshments. The little kiosk I remembered was gone, but the linden tree, gate, and sign were still there. Auschwitz had become an international tourist attraction and museum. There was guide service, but I knew what I was looking at. So the three of us chose to go alone, and walked by ourselves through the block houses to see the exhibits, although the camp had many visitors that day all trying not to get in each other's way. The changes from 1965 made me feel detached from what I remembered. What I had learned about wartime Poland and Auschwitz since my first visit only reenforced and enriched my memory. The crowds, the tour guides, the atmosphere of people being on a day's outing all contributed to a feeling of ordinariness in this extraordinary place. That upset me because I realized time was eroding the memory and the horror of this place. In 1965 the war had ended only 20 years before and the brutality of Auschwitz was still fresh in our minds.

Our driver took us for the short ride to the Birkenau camp and parked outside the main gate. By this time there was bus transportation between the camps, which had not been available in 1965. Until this visit I had imagined Birkenau from films, novels, and memoirs. As we walked through the gate now, I saw for the first time the railway tracks and the simple siding where arrivals were selected for work or death and where their belongings were left and later sorted by the "trustee" prisoners. From that gate I looked out onto a huge field surrounded by wire that enclosed rows of barrack-like buildings—some crumbling, some only a concrete floor, and others intact—into which we ventured. They contained the layers of barren bunks and the small stove that barely heated the hut. At the far end of this field were the remnants of two Zyklon B showers and furnaces where visitors had left flowers and wreaths. Before abandoning the camp and forcing the surviving prisoners to march west toward Germany, the Nazis blew up the crematoria in an attempt to cover up their atrocities. Between those ruins stood the International Monument to Victims of Fascism erected in 1967. We were silent and shaken, each of us alone walking about and looking. On the steps of the monument were clusters of young people, many from Israel and others from the United States, Australia, Europe, even South America, making their Holocaust pilgrimage. Some sang Hebrew and Yiddish songs, the boys wore yarmulkes, and many of the young people had a Star of David or a country patch on their back packs. I wondered what those young people were thinking and experiencing in this terrible place and was moved by their pilgrimage. I was also overwhelmed by the vastness of Birkenau, and, as in Auschwitz more than 30 years ago, I felt ghosts all around me. Haunted is perhaps too aesthetic a word to describe how I felt that lovely afternoon—I was sick at heart.

Much had changed at Auschwitz since 1965, but Birkenau seemed untouched by any "improvements." It was the authentic, grim reminder of what man had wrought on man in this now holy place. We returned to Kraków in the late afternoon subdued by our visit. The irony of the name of the town Oświęcim struck me for the first time: "place of light" and "enlightenment."

IN THE FALL OF 2010, toward the end of a short trip with an American couple to Vienna and Lwów, we flew to Kraków. We were tracing the wife's Jewish roots, and I encouraged them to visit Kraków to explore its Jewish heritage, especially in the Kazimierz district, and to visit a medieval city left intact in spite of Nazi occupation. The husband said he would like to go to Auschwitz, so he and I hired a driver from our hotel. The drive was short and I could see how European Union money had rebuilt the country's roads. I was amazed by the new buildings and prosperous farms we saw along the way. I could have been driving though Ohio and not the Kraków suburbs I saw in 1998.

We parked in the same lot as in 1998 but now there were even more cars and buses from all over Europe. No longer could we enter the camp without being part of a large group led by a guide, and, as is customary in most museums today, members of the group were offered headphones for the tour. This time, out of curiosity about the presentation, I refused to take the headphones. We bought our tickets and waited with a group of about twenty for our tour to begin. One chose a tour according to the language in which it would be conducted. A young man introduced himself and got our tour underway. He was well versed in the camp lore and kept up a steady stream of information.

Large groups came and went, chatting, sipping tea and coffee, and eating candy bars or fruit. For some, the visit was clearly not a tour, judging from the anguish on their faces, but I saw few such people that day. Our guide gave the group a minute or two to look at the exhibits and then filed us past the next group coming through the corridor. He answered questions while quietly urging us to keep moving as quickly as possible to make room for the next group. I felt the kind of objectivity that one finds in any museum of historic artifacts. But these were about torture, starvation, medical experimentation, death.

There were changes in Block 11. During a recent renovation, two more suffocation cells had been discovered in the walls and were now exposed for viewing. Most startling to me was that the worn doorsill to the execution yard had been replaced by a solid stone and the courtyard was cleaned up and painted. It struck me as a stage set, not an execution chamber. What had been palpable horror had been neatened up so that one no longer had a sense that people were actually murdered here.

A bus now transported each group from Auschwitz to Birkenau, then back to the museum entrance. Birkenau remained unchanged since my last visit, which threw the changes at Auschwitz into high relief.

As I walked through both camps this time, my anger at their gentrification softened. How valuable, even under these organized conditions, seeing Auschwitz-Birkenau was for anyone who chose to come here. Seeing the camps would not ensure that such atrocities would not happen again—and we know they have happened throughout the world. However, looking at the stark reality of what is left in these camps and learning something of what happened in them gives me hope that more people may come to respect and honor each other's humanness and assuage their cruelty. As distressing as the new Auschwitz-Birkenau museum is to me, I can appreciate that it has made it possible to accommodate and inform so many more people who visit this monumental example of man's inhumanity to man. Although I am grateful for what I learned and the affecting way I learned it in 1965, I will, in any case, encourage others to make their own pilgrimages to these places, however the presentation of these camps has evolved. ◇

Finisterre

Sophia G. Starmack

There's only one heart at the end of the world.
Sea wind dirties your hair,
comes back with salt fingers for my mouth.

Your father writes, *please come home*
and tell me if you've had a religious experience.
We're tourists, squatting in the dust under the lighthouse
to pour out the last of the bottle.

Beyond the horizon, a thousand ships
sailing off the edge of time.
We cannot see them.
Maybe you can tell your father this:
The curve of the world unravels like a silver thread.
The heart, the eye of the needle. ◇

Waking

Sophia G. Starmack

The man on the park bench
is licking his tattoos.

He's got a bundle of sharpened sticks,
rags, old *Watchtower* pages,
dog-eared books,
a tiny neon flashlight,
all pulled from his outsize jacket.

He traces the sticks over his skin,
digging in a little: no blood,
but his tongue is quick,
a pink kitten, and he's got
one straight-shooting eye
and one that's unhinged.

When I was a child they told me
Ezekiel ate the scroll
in his greed for the Word,
and Isaiah babbled while the city raged
at the sores on his buttocks and thighs,
but I'm watching this man,
with one eye on the exit,

watching for a knife, a shot, a needle,
steeling one arm around my purse
and hating myself:
hating myself.
I have never been so small. ◇

New Rochelle's Jonathan Tropper
An Interview

Joan Motyka

B EING A NOVELIST, JONATHAN TROPPER SAYS, "IS MY DAY JOB."
But as his sixth novel, *One Last Thing Before I Go*, was making its way into bookstores in August, he was traveling between Westchester, where he lives, and North Carolina, where he was working on the HBO/Cinemax TV show, *Banshee*, as co-creator and executive producer.

And working on a screenplay for 20th Century Fox.

And submitting outlines for another screenplay, an adaptation of *One Last Thing Before I Go*, which he's writing for Paramount.

And gearing up for the marketing of his novel.

Oh, and trying to figure out his next novel.

This is what the writing life looks like for Jonathan Tropper these days.

Mr. Tropper, whose books have been translated into more than 20 languages, had a breakout success with his 2009 novel *This Is Where I Leave You*. With more than 200,000 copies sold, it was named best book of the year by *The Washington Post*, NPR, *The Los Angeles Times*, and Amazon, among others. It made its way to *The New York Times* bestseller list, was picked up by Warner Brothers, and is now in development.

"Few can rival his poignant depictions of damaged men befuddled by the women they love," *Kirkus Review* said of him.

One of Tropper's damaged men is Silver, the main character in his latest book, *One Last Thing Before I Go*. A divorced drummer, with a one-hit-wonder single well behind him, he plays in wedding bands and hangs around with other divorced men as adrift as he. As his ex-wife prepares to remarry and his teenaged daughter confides in him that she is pregnant, Silver learns that he needs emergency lifesaving heart surgery—and these events all prompt him to wonder: What is his life worth to those he has loved so poorly?

"Tropper gets men," *USA Today* said.

He also gets families, particularly dysfunctional suburban ones, and writes about them with a breeziness and hard-edged humor that illuminate the angst beneath them all.

In late summer, the 42-year-old Mr. Tropper sat down with the *The Westchester Review* to talk about his characters, his books, and, especially, the writing life. What follows is an edited transcript.

You've been in North Carolina working on your TV show and you've got other writing projects going. What's all the juggling like?
After I finished editing my novel I worked on an episode of the show, which is called *Banshee*. It's about a thief who gets out of jail after 15 years, steals an identity, and becomes the sheriff of a small Pennsylvania town.

Writing for TV is very intense. We write as we go and there's a tremendous amount of rewriting. I just finished the last episode and there was a month of intense rewriting. I've been writing nonstop for the show.

I'm also in the middle of rewriting a screenplay for Fox, called *Kodachrome*. It's about a father and son's troubled relationship and it's set against the backdrop of the end of Kodachrome. It's set in the last week you could ever get Kodachrome film processed, at the last plant in the world doing it, in Kansas. People from all around the world came to get their last rolls developed.

How do your novels fit in with all of this?
My goal is to start another book. I always want to be writing a book, no matter what else I'm doing. Being a novelist is my day job.

What's the new novel about?
I don't have an idea yet for the next one.

Is that worrisome?
There are always a few months when I think I know what I'm writing but I really don't. When I start I know about the overall parts of the book but not its particulars. That early part is about finding a voice, finding the characters. I throw out a little at the beginning. I might know a family or a character but the plot doesn't come until I spend time on it.

Are you throwing out less now, as you have written more books and tackled so many other writing projects?
No. It's part of my writing process. When I didn't know what I was doing, I'd sit and not write. Now I've trained myself to produce pages. On a good day I'd like to net 10 pages, maybe generate 20 pages. Once I hit my groove I can generate a chapter or two in a day—a chapter or two that's worth keeping.

How long does it take you to write a book?
The last book, *One Last Thing Before I Go,* took way too long, about two years. But it wasn't all straight writing; there were a lot of interruptions. If I'm writing steadily, it takes me about a year, maybe 18 months.

How about revising?
In the last book, I did a lot of rewriting. I wrote it over a longer period of time than usual so I spent a lot of time massaging the voice and making it consistent. When you rewrite over time, you find the places where you've repeated yourself, or where the character changes direction. I do a continuity pass so that it's all of a piece.

And other things can change too. In an earlier draft of that book, I had a lot more of Silver actually saying what was on his mind, actually expressing what he was thinking without realizing he was doing it. But I didn't want to lean on that technique so much and I toned it down.

Do you like revising?

I like the creative part in the rewriting. When I speak to aspiring writers I say that the difference between a writer who's had success and one who hasn't is that if you know what you're doing, you can spend a year just to rewrite.

How do you know when to stop rewriting?

If I didn't have a deadline I'd revise and never let it go. I'm always trying to find ways to refine the writing.

Is it difficult to jump from one project to another?

I like creative diversification. I love the idea of a visual story, a screenplay. There are just different muscles you use when you're writing prose, when you are sitting all day long by yourself writing a book.

I like being able to work on a novel, say from nine to two. With a screenplay I can be productive for a few more hours after lunch.

As you work on various projects, do you prefer one kind of writing over another?

Instinctually I'm more of a prose writer. What I love about writing a book is that every word is mine. From the idea to publication, it's all me. In film, it's all collaboration. But right now for me this is all a happy mix.

You were also teaching writing. Are you still doing that?

No. I stopped teaching. There's no time. I was at Manhattanville for about four years.

What did you want your students to take away from your classes?

I don't think you can teach someone to write but you can teach them to refine their work and to learn how to critique their work. I wanted my students to read. You can't be a writer if you're not constantly reading.

I also wanted them to feel that it's not impossible to make writing your life. I'm not an intellectual heavyweight. They're doing at 20 more than I ever did then. I wanted them to know it is a matter of perseverance and passion and some degree of ability.

What are you reading?
The last book I read was *The First Husband* by Laura Dave. It's a fantastic and uncomfortable look at relationships.

In book after book, you certainly tackle relationships. There's a lot of craziness in the families you portray. How do you think about these families?
First I imagine the overall tone of the family. Every family has a tone. For the Foxtons in *This Is Where I Leave You*, for example, I wanted a tone that was defensive verbalizing with a lot of one-upmanship. There are a lot of walls between those characters. When they're together, they're on their guard, and that informs how everyone talks to each other. The mother was the one who pushed through all of that. That family had been broken a long time ago. They lost the ability for sustained communication and for them to have to communicate, as they were sitting shivah for seven days for the father in the book, that led to a lot of tension.

But so often your tension is tempered by humor.
To the extent that it's conscious, when you're writing about difficult topics, if you bury the reader in dense hyper-articulate prose, something gets lost. And sometimes it's the reader's attention that gets lost. Writers can belabor a moment too much. I like writers like Richard Russo, John Irving, Jonathan Leithem, Joyce Carol Oates, who turn a fantastic phrase but they don't disappear behind a wall of words.

Writing humor is hard. How does the humor come to you?
You can't look at any aspect of the human condition and not find elements of humor. Even in sadness, you can find the humor. No matter what's happening, there are random moments that are not to be repeated—and I take pleasure in finding those moments. I think our brains

work on many levels. Like when you find your wife kissing someone and you're thinking about picking up the dry cleaning. When you read something like that, maybe you think: I might do that too.

There's also a lot of sex in your books, in addition to humor.
A lot? I don't know what you read, but I don't think there's so much. I wouldn't think Philip Roth or Updike or John Irving would think there's much sex in my books. But having sex in the books does make for interesting conversation with the people you know. When people know you, it's the thing they home in on —and I'm really anticipating this when my TV show comes out.

The thing is, when you're writing about middle-aged men going through crises, no way that sex can't play a role. But I've never written to titillate. I think of sex as part of the tapestry of these men's lives.

Talking seems to be part of the tapestry too. Your books contain a lot of great dialog. Sometime there are real zingers, sometimes poignant comments, sometimes you use language that keys a reader to the fact that a character is lying, or unable to express what he's really thinking.
The dialog is why I was invited to write screenplays. I take tremendous pleasure in using dialogue to illuminate characters. I want you to *know* characters by the way they speak.

And I'm really interested in nonverbal parts of relationships, where there is a closeness or an animosity between characters that develops *in spite* of dialogue. I want you to get a sense of what's happening behind the dialogue. In *One Last Thing Before I Go*, Silver is a guy nobody else in the book should like—but they don't want to get rid of him. So there must be something there, in Silver.

With Silver, there's a lot of internal dialogue—the things we know Silver's thinking, and what he's actually saying, and in the book, the two cross over, one into the other quite often, because of his medical problems. How did you think about that internal and external dialogue?

Silver's a man who's like a bystander to the wreck of his own life and he's powerless to do anything about it. I love a character who has fallen silent in his own life—and then who becomes just the opposite: articulate. It's very liberating to a man like that to open up the way he did, actually speaking what was on his mind, even though because of his medical condition he wasn't quite aware he was doing it. Maybe we'd all like a one-day pass to do that.

Your male characters are so often flawed men—the kind of men you wouldn't want your daughter to marry—and yet at some point in the book we start liking them, understanding something about them.
I always try to make them honest. These men can be incredibly troubled but if there's honesty about their faults, that humanizes them. In *The Book of Joe* my character was a jerk. It was an incredible journey for him to take to get to the end. Editors wanted him to be sympathetic; people who sell and market the work are always worried that the main character has to be sympathetic. But I disagree that that sells a book. I think major characters can be sympathetic in their failures and their flaws. I think people will empathize and sympathize with that, particularly seeing the characters come through their flaws to the other side.

Your most recent book, *One Last Thing Before I Go,* was different from those that came before it in that you have several people telling their stories, a shifting point of view.
I made a conscious decision to move away from first person, and to be less confessional. As much as I love writing confessional, I don't want the books to start sounding the same. I wanted to work on a slightly broader canvas with shifting points of view. I wanted to get into different heads. It's liberating to fall into different voices, and I'd like to move more toward that. I loved going between Silver and his ex-wife Denise and their daughter, Casey. I focused on the trio—Silver, Denise and Casey —and had one sympathetic character, Rich, the man Denise was marrying. Everybody viewed Rich in the same way—that he was a nice guy caught up in their craziness. He was the stable presence among them.

What would be a hard character for you to write?
Maybe writing from the point of view of a woman as a main character. Something in me doesn't move to do it. "Owning" a woman's character—making a woman the principal character—I'd have to have a deep understanding, maybe a deeper understanding of women than I have. It's been okay for me to do some of that—writing from the perspective of Denise and Casey—but not the whole main character

What about place in your writing—the setting for all that goes on? I know you live in New Rochelle. Some of your books refer to places in Westchester or are renamed but feel very Westchester.
I like that, without having to think about it, I have a full understanding of the place my characters are in—the Hudson Valley, the East Coast—I know I can breathe life into it effortlessly. The location becomes a minor character of the book and I don't want to think I'm not getting it right.

You've clearly worked to get things right. So for you now, what's the best thing about being a writer?
It keeps me out of an office, and having to get a nine-to-five job and a boss. I wasn't cut out for that. And I love the artistry of writing, of trying to express and articulate things in a meaningful way. ◇

Geisha in the Mirror

Michael Carman

Her chalk cheeks erase the white
paper she's not drawn
on—she's less
than nothing, a single fine-penned line,

idea of perfection.
One ear, one nostril,
two blank eyes,
fluted swirl of her silk kimono

binding, watercolor-washed—
sky-blue like herons,
pink like sky.
Still, her heart beats beneath deathly white,

while only two vermilions—
mouth, hairbow—call out
like pippins
nesting in pagodas of her hair.

She's in the mirror, nowhere else.
Nothing but imagination there. ◇

Passing

Jeffrey W. Peterson

"Irene studied the lovely creature standing beside her for some clue to her identity.
Who could she be? Where and when had they met?
. . . She didn't mind not being recognized."
Nella Larsen, *Passing*

They always say my momma's
just passing—
    and they always say she's
    just passing—
but my momma's got that
blackberry blood.

She ain't trying to gentrify
gentrify—
    ain't nobody ever gentrify
    gentrify—
and why would she anyway
if she can't spell it?

My moms will beat you fast
if you calls her—
    she'll beat you so fast
    if you call her out.
My moms ain't euro,
redskin, or spic. ◇

Dinner with
the Grahams

Jonathan Vatner

"**I** AM DELIGHTED TO FINALLY MEET YOU!"
   Peter slapped my shoulder to emphasize each of the last three words, then lunged upon me in a ravenous embrace, nearly pushing me back out the front door. I barely had time to reach my left hand behind me to spare the bouquet I had brought as a hostess gift. I tried patting his back to keep things platonic, but he squeezed, rubbed, then squeezed again, as though determined to arouse me. He stepped back and looked me up and down. "I can see why Anthony loved you. You are just too scrumptious." He scrubbed my cheek with his fuzzy knuckles.

He was a tidier, more attractive version of his younger brother, Anthony, whom I had once known intimately. He had Anthony's Alexandrian nose—though his had a dignified bump on the bridge—and Anthony's hair, though thicker on top and graying at the sides. His tightly wrought body was sheathed in a fitted sport jacket that bulged oddly in the lapels; maybe he had a lot in his pockets.

"How was the ride?" he asked, guiding me into the house. "I hope Roger didn't bother you with his political garbage." Peter had insisted on sending his Mercedes and I can't say I minded the luxury.

"Actually, we listened to NPR the whole time."

He laughed. "Don't tell me you're as bad as he is."

A statuesque woman glided into view. Her skin was pale and her features soft; gentle wrinkles, fond memories of sunlight, lay about her face. Her white cotton dress featured an ample décolletage, perhaps even a sliver of nipple, and I was slightly embarrassed to find myself staring. "Welcome," she said, her eyelids drooping demurely.

"This is my wife, Trudie. Trudie, this is Jeremiah. He and Anthony were lovers."

That description seemed off—my memories of our relationship played like a TV series I had watched as a child, not as felt experience—but it was true, we'd been desperately in love for a few wild months after I graduated from college. I hadn't seen him since walking out on him fifteen years before, and I couldn't blame him for ignoring my weepy phone calls. We had fought after he snorted too much cocaine, and though I'd been sure he was going to be fine, that he was just being dramatic, he saw my exit as the ultimate betrayal.

So it was a surprise earlier that week when Peter called to tell me that Anthony had bequeathed me the cabin, the one where we spent almost our whole relationship, the one that Anthony had said he bought for me—though I had assumed our breakup annulled all his vows. Since then, I married Phoebe, my soul mate in ways that Anthony could never be, except that our bodies didn't fit together quite as seamlessly.

"This is for you," I said, holding out the twenty-dollar mixed bouquet, realizing too late how shamefully outclassed the sapless carnations and alstroemeria looked in their home. At least I hadn't brought wine. Anthony never drank anything under a hundred dollars a bottle.

"Thank you," Trudie said, with more heart than the flowers deserved. "The table is already far too crowded, so I'll put these in a nice vase in the kitchen. I hope you won't mind."

"Not at all." I was relieved not to have to see them.

"What'll you have to drink?" Peter asked. "You look like a Scotch kind of guy. Give him the grand tour, Trudie." He left us in the foyer.

An enormous chandelier, overflowing with droplets of crystal, hung above us. A dark glossy balustrade swept upward from my left, leading to a balcony that encircled us completely. In the center of the room stood a round mahogany table, topped with a Chinese vase piled high with silk flowers.

"Your home is spectacular," I said.

"We like to think so." Trudie spoke without opening her jaw, which forced her lips into a pout and showed off teeth as glossy as Peter's.

We walked through a series of rooms, each grander than the last. Beyond the living room and sunroom we reached the dining room. A long table was set for three at one end, with gold-rimmed chargers and a battalion of wine glasses. An etched crystal pitcher, filled with ice water, looked familiar. In a tall brass candelabrum, several tapers burned, painting the walls with a flickering light bolstered by a fire on the hearth. A tasteful Chinese urn, about the size of a coconut, was alone on the fireplace mantel. Two windows on the far wall were dark; I moved close to the obsidian surface and made out a lawn stretching downward to an ink-black forest.

"Would it be all right to see more of the house after dinner?" I asked, caught up in the thrill of mansion porn.

"Oh, no," said Trudie. "You've seen everything."

It was obvious that we hadn't completed the loop of rooms on the first floor, not to mention going upstairs. "So the rest is private?" I asked.

"You don't want to see the rest," Peter said, appearing with my Scotch. "Now, shall we?"

We sat, he at the head of the table, I at his left facing Trudie, to his right. She smiled at me vacantly. I swigged my drink.

A plump young woman in black pants and a white sateen blouse emerged from behind a swinging door, carrying a corked bottle in each hand. "Riesling or Merlot?" she asked me, and when I hesitated, added, "White or red?"

"It's a good Merlot, not like anything you've had," Peter cut in. "That poor grape has gotten such a bad name in this country."

"What are you serving?" I wasn't a purist about matching the wine to the color of the meat, but I worried about seeming unrefined by not asking.

"Squab wrapped in pancetta," said Trudie. "You would do well with either."

"Trudie's cooking is marvelous," said Peter.

It sounded heavy to me. "I guess I'll take that Merlot, then."

"Excellent choice," Peter said, as the server poured. "Trudie, my dear?"

"Riesling, please."

"Riesling for me, too, Lizzie. Jeremiah, this is no trap. You have chosen better than we: the Merlot really is a grand vin. But Trudie and I have been drinking red all day like a pair of hopeless lushes. We need the white to wake us out of our stupor."

I laughed at his frail joke.

"We've only had a few glasses," Trudie corrected. "Don't give our guest the wrong idea."

"But we do love getting nice and drunk, don't we?"

Trudie touched her husband's hand, communicating a mixture of affection and warning. "You more than I, dear."

All of this was performed quickly, the lines spilling over each other. They were showing off—and we had barely mentioned Anthony—yet I was pleased to be a witness.

Peter sniffed and swirled his wine, then took a sip. "This one is magnificent, Trudie."

"If there's one thing you can say about Peter, it's that he buys only the best wine," Trudie remarked, tipping the glass to her lips.

"Yes, the Graham fortune resides mostly in our livers."

I found myself laughing alone. I too swirled my wine and took a sip. It was full-bodied and smooth, fruity but subtle. I hadn't tasted wine like that since my dinners with Anthony, three-hour affairs in restaurants so exclusive their names weren't posted outside. "Very good. Very good."

Lizzie returned with salad plates, a mountain of frisée with walnuts, dried cherries, and crumbled Gorgonzola.

"Bon appetit!" Trudie exclaimed, and our forks descended in concert.

Before I had taken a bite, Peter said, "Trudie spent all day at the farmers' market. She's a master shopper."

She interrupted a sip of wine. "But I didn't spend all day, just an hour or so. The way Peter tells it, I'm some sort of a perfectionist freak."

"She's always downplaying her efforts," he said. "Take anything she says and multiply it by five."

"I despise you," she told him, with a wink aimed at me. I pretended not to see it. I had always hated the forced intimacy of winks; only Anthony had succeeded at them, probably because I lapped up every intimacy he offered.

"Can we talk about Anthony?" I asked, afraid I was breaking a house rule: no serious talk until the main course was served. "I don't know if . . . "

"Of course, of course. My poor brother," said Peter. "Such a surprise."

"A tragedy," Trudie added.

"Can I ask what happened?"

Peter lifted his hands in surrender. "What's there to say? It was a heart attack. Someone called 911. He was dead before the ambulance arrived."

"Did he have a heart problem?"

"Runs in the family, I'm afraid. Trudie won't let me go a day without exercise."

She turned to me and raised her eyebrows. "Doctor's orders, not mine."

"Yes, but who picked the doctor?" He directed a series of faux-hostile air kisses at her.

"Where was he when he died?" I asked.

"In his San Francisco house. Did he have that when you were together? Frankly, and I'm sorry to admit this, I don't remember which one you were. He must have had . . . how many boyfriends would you say he had, Trudie?"

"Hundreds." She flipped a hand in the air in exasperation.

"He was fond of telling us that he had found 'the one,'" he added with a smirk.

Their offhand comments hewed me. I had assumed he had dated since we broke up, not that he had cycled through men. Now I wondered even more how, out of the multitudes, Anthony could have chosen me to accept his cabin. "We dated in ninety-four," I said, with as much composure as possible. "In New York."

"Really? You must have been memorable, then. I thought you were more recent." He meant it jovially, but still I felt diminished. "He moved to San Francisco a little after that."

"Beautiful place," said Trudie. "Painted lady in Noe Valley. That light . . . " She trailed off in a reverie.

"Has there been a funeral?"

Peter nodded. "Two weeks ago. I'm sorry we didn't know to invite you. We didn't get the will until last week and then it took some time to find you."

"We held the ceremony here, in the backyard," Trudie said. "It was lovely—as lovely as a funeral could be—but I think the pastor was drunk. He just went on and on about nothing."

"It wasn't nothing, dear, it was God." He turned to me. "We asked him specifically not to do the 'Our Father' shtick."

Even to me, who would have been an atheist had I cared whether or not God existed, they sounded awfully callous. "And where is he buried?" I asked, fearing suddenly that they might have tossed him into a hole in the backyard.

"Oh, he's not buried. He's up there." Trudie pointed to the Chinese urn on the mantel. "For now."

My gut lurched. "His ashes?"

Peter put his hand on my forearm, both a balm and a manacle. "We don't believe in burial, but he didn't leave any directions on where he wanted to go. We figured we would know when we found the place. For now, he's keeping us company up there."

It seemed inhuman to keep Anthony in a jar in the dining room, and yet it meant that his remains were right in front of me. Without knowing what ritual I was performing, I walked to the mantel, lifted the urn and felt its weight in my hands. All of Anthony, his broad shoulders and generosity of muscle, his sensuality and rage, had been cooked down to this. Somehow it wasn't their right to reduce him in this way.

"May I?" I asked, and they nodded. I plucked off the top; inside was a clear plastic bag half full of bone-colored dust, the texture of fine sand. I didn't know what I'd been expecting, but this was a painful disappointment. I closed the container, replaced it on the mantel, and sat back down, just as Lizzie entered to clear our plates.

"Would you like some more wine?" Trudie asked.

I was too flustered to respond. She poured me a full glass anyway, and filled everyone's goblet with water from the pitcher, which looked more familiar as the evening progressed. Could it have been Anthony's? No matter how vigorously I plumbed our history, the memory wouldn't surface. "It's a beautiful pitcher," I said.

"Yes, isn't it?" Trudie gushed. "This is the first time we've used it."

"Do you know if Anthony owned a similar piece?" I was feeling aggressive, perhaps as revenge for what they did to Anthony.

Peter responded. "Ah, so you recognize it! He loved to entertain, didn't he? We put most of his things in storage, for the estate sale. But Trudie has always loved that pitcher, so we took it."

Lizzie entered again with two plates of squab and placed them in front of Trudie and me, then stole back to the kitchen for the third. The tiny bird, clothed in a crispy gown of bacon, was perched atop a hill of mashed potatoes, bits of the ruddy skins visible on the surface. As delicious as it looked, it was hard to think about food with Anthony so close. But social graces required me to eat along with them, and my discomfort in their company sped my fork.

The phone rang. Peter flashed an irritated smile and, excusing himself, left the room.

Trudie and I ate in silence. I was about to compliment the food when she asked, "How have you made out over the years? Have you found a special guy?"

"I'm married. To a woman." I was relieved to set the record straight.

"Wonderful!" she said, the machinations visible in her eyes. "Why didn't you invite her?"

"She wasn't free," I lied. In reality, I hadn't wanted her to come. She didn't belong to my past life.

"Well, we could have postponed."

Peter reappeared and sat down. Trudie turned to him and, with stronger enunciation than I would have preferred, said, "Next time, we'll have to invite Jeremiah's wife, too."

Peter couldn't conceal his surprise. He proceeded slowly, as if being careful not to offend me. "Oh, what's her name?"

"Phoebe."

"And when were you married?"

"It was twelve years in January."

"So Phoebe has . . . come to terms with your past?"

"Peter!" Trudie scolded.

"Yeah, yeah," I said, though in truth I had never told her. I almost did a few times before we got married, but she seemed happier not knowing. And then the secret was entombed under the steady pile of years. I still hadn't figure out how, or if, I would introduce the cabin to her. I had thought about keeping it as a private respite, like taking a lover. But Phoebe adored the mountains; perhaps there was a way to introduce it without mentioning Anthony.

"Well," Peter concluded, grinning, "you sure gave up some nice disposable income. Being married is fine and all, but this one can be a bit pricey sometimes."

Trudie gave him a playful nudge. I could have explained that I was a poorly paid freelance writer and Phoebe handled our mortgage, or that my health insurance came courtesy of her teaching job, but in their presence, I sensed that mentioning Phoebe's income might again break a rule.

We finished our dinners. Lizzie upended the bottle into my wine glass until the final dark purple droplets rolled off the lip. I don't remember her clearing the plates or bringing in dessert; I was experiencing sensory overload, not just from the wine but from the whirligig of conversation, the heavy food, and the grandeur of the house itself. A distracting buzz filled my ears.

Dessert was a peach-mango tarte tatin, glistening in the candlelight. The tarte tatin—upended at the last moment to expose its delectable underbelly—was Anthony's favorite dessert, and it seemed that its presence was no mistake. A dollop of whipped cream had been placed on the side, a mint leaf sprouting from its flocculent skin. When no one was looking, I swiped a white dab with my finger. Its texture was firm, beaten almost to butter—just the way I liked it.

Lizzie appeared with coffee and a slim bottle of ice wine. She filled our glasses and mugs.

Raising his glass, Peter said, "To Jeremiah, for what we hope will be the first of a long tradition of dinners at our home."

Would I really be dining so elegantly again? The thick, sweet wine burned like whiskey.

Peter excused himself for a moment and returned with a manila envelope that he presented to me with a benevolent smile. Undoing the tie took an eternity. I slid out the contents, two pages and a handful of keys. I scanned the copy of the deed. My eye caught Anthony's signature, a high hump and two low ones, more like an EKG than a name, and lingered over those curves, remembering his hand and those weighty pens with ink that poured out of the tips. My signature, similar to my current one but less confident, was below his.

"Now, Jeremiah," said Peter, suddenly serious, "there's something we need to talk about before you go. I hesitated to bring it up while we were enjoying dinner . . . I'm guessing you were a little, well, surprised that Anthony left his cabin to you?"

I nodded carefully.

"The short explanation is, he didn't; there was a mistake. His original will, which he updated every few years, left the cabin to his boyfriend of the moment. And the will itself was a mess. His estate would have spent years in probate. Anthony called me a few years back about this. He had finally accepted that he would never find true love, and realized it would be best to keep the cabin in the family so the next generation of Grahams would be able to enjoy it. I helped him draw up a new, stronger will that left it to our family. It was the fairest thing possible, and we all thought the will was airtight."

I had sensed this moment would arrive based on their smug confidence. Why else would they have invited me to dinner unless they wanted something from me? But though I began dinner skeptical that Anthony had meant for the cabin to go to me, now it was devastating to hear that he hadn't. Worse than losing the cabin was parting with the idea that he had loved me through fifteen years of silence.

"Apparently, it wasn't airtight," Peter continued, as Trudie sipped her wine. "Although the will clearly states, with his signature, that the cabin should remain in the family, the deed to the property said something different. As you remember, Anthony was a hopeless romantic.

When he bought the cabin, I'm sure he was completely certain that you two would always be together, and he listed you as a joint owner on the deed. But then he promptly forgot about it. Well, it's really my fault for trusting him when he said he was certain that the deed was clean. What I'm trying to say is that, as these things go, deed trumps will."

I was speechless. It was all a big accident, a slip of the pen forgotten beneath the landslide of time. I should have known that the cabin was just another of Anthony's self-terminating promises, like the one he had spun the night I met him: "No matter what happens with us, I can tell we're going to be best friends as long as we live."

"What do you think?" asked Peter.

"I . . . I guess that makes sense." Speaking made me aware of just how drunk I had become; my tongue could barely push the words out.

Peter, whose stony eyes in that moment revealed perfect sobriety, reached into his breast pocket and produced a pen and an unsealed envelope containing two folded sheets of paper. "Then if you wouldn't mind signing this, we'll right the error without any further ado." The pen made a muffled clink as he placed it on the table in front of me.

It was a contract in duplicate, written in the simplest possible language: I was agreeing that the will would take precedence over the deed. It seemed completely justified. And yet, through the thickening haze, I knew something wasn't right. It was an indefinable sense that the night had proceeded too smoothly, that every word of conversation had been planned, that he had waited for the alcohol to soften me before the reveal. Something was off about Peter's tidy composure so soon after the death of his brother, and Anthony's pitcher, pilfered from the cabin—still officially my cabin—and used without ceremony or apology, and a deed that no one had bothered to double-check. I did believe that my inheritance had been a mistake, but maybe that wasn't the whole story.

My stomach began to churn. I had to get up from that table. I would use the bathroom and then I would think this through. Yes, the bathroom. I looked up at Peter and started to push my chair back.

He reached forward as if to catch me. "Of course, we want to compensate you for your troubles, make this a windfall for you. To that end, if it would be all right with you, we'd like to give you this." He pulled a folded check from his pants pocket and placed it on top of the contract.

I had to squint to count the zeroes. Five thousand dollars. It might have been a fair deal if the cabin really wasn't mine, but I couldn't trust myself to decide anything right then. "I'm just going to use the bathroom for a minute. My wife tells me not to make any decisions on a full bladder." Fabrication, I believed, had no loose ends; it could not be breached.

"Oh, sure," said Peter, hastily. "It's right off the foyer."

I returned to the front of the house. The bathroom was a traditional water closet, an oak-paneled tank above my head, attached to the toilet with a brass pipe. I sat on the toilet seat cover and took a deep breath, already more sober. I was sure they were hiding something upstairs. Even if they weren't, poking around up there—doing anything to loosen the bonds of decorum—might give me a sense of control in a situation where I was out of my depth.

Keeping an eye out, I crept up the stairs and opened a door. It was another bathroom, larger than the one downstairs. I tried a few more doors until I found the master bedroom. In Peter's closet I recognized one of Anthony's suits; indeed, his initials, "ARG" (apt, I had always thought) were monogrammed on the inside pocket. Anthony had told me that the suit was hand-sewn in Italy for $8,000. Apparently Peter brought it into his wardrobe less than two weeks after his brother's death.

I opened the drawers in the bureau and found, inside the bottom one, a clutter of Anthony's things: a small wooden box that held a Rolex I recognized and a few gold rings, a copper-bottomed saucepan, six half-ounce tubes of medical-grade face cream, and three etched glasses that matched his pitcher. I was certain that Peter had stolen all of these valuables from the cabin.

Staring at this plunder, I remembered where Anthony had gotten the pitcher. Peter had sent the set for Anthony's twenty-sixth birthday. We were on the porch when the UPS truck arrived. "From a distance, he can be a nice guy," Anthony had said. I asked what he meant by "from a distance," and he explained that they hadn't talked since he was in college. I had vaguely remembered that he was estranged from his family, but it hadn't occurred to me that he hated them.

An appealing fantasy flitted by. Was it possible that Anthony had known about the deed and had hidden it from his brother? It wasn't likely—foremost because although he hated Peter, he also hated me in the end—but the possibility emboldened me, and the sum total of my understanding assured me of one thing: I wasn't going to give up the cabin until I could prove that it wasn't meant to be mine.

I hurried downstairs, leaning heavily on the banister to hush my footfalls. Peter was waiting in the foyer.

"We were worried about you," he said.

"Oh, you don't need to worry about me," I replied, anxiety dampening my words.

"I thought we mentioned that upstairs was off-limits."

"I'm sorry; I was just admiring the chandelier from the balcony."

He grunted, then added casually, "You'll have to come back again. We were just talking about how much we've been enjoying our time with you." He slapped my shoulder hard enough to sting and led me back into the dining room.

The contract, along with that leaden pen, was waiting at my place at the table. I didn't sit down. "I hope it's all right with you, but I want to take a few days to think about this whole thing. I'm sure I'll decide to hand it over, but my wife—there she goes again—tells me not to make any big decisions without a good night's sleep." I attempted a laugh; it could have been mistaken for a cry.

Peter studied me. "I'd prefer to settle this now."

"It's not good to cross her. She has an annoying tendency to be right." This wasn't exactly true. She certainly was right more than I, but she never would have lorded that fact over me. Yet in the moment, the marriage cliché—the supposedly amusing idea of a wife emasculating her husband behind closed doors—seemed like the only lie that could rescue me, the only one that could give me equal footing with them.

"I don't think it's up to her really," Peter said. "Let's just get this over with, so we can avoid any unpleasantness."

"I'd much rather wait."

"You haven't seen him in fifteen years, Jeremiah. Face it, he didn't want his most prized possession to go to you."

"I can't be sure he wanted it to go to you, either."

"He was my brother."

"I think I'll be going now," I said, snatching my jacket from the chair. "Thank you for dinner."

He pulled out a legal-size envelope from his breast pocket and handed it to Lizzie, who appeared from behind me to take it. She in turn placed it in my hands. She was the only person in the room without any stake in the cabin, the only person who could legally give this to me, I realized, as the contents of the envelope became clear to me.

Peter's lapels no longer buckled. "I'm frankly disappointed in you, Jeremiah. We could have done this in a much more civilized way. Consider yourself served."

I stared at the envelope, numb with rage. I couldn't bring myself to speak. I had to get out of that house, away from those Grahams. No wonder Anthony had broken off the contact. Now I was sure that the cabin, and Anthony, were mine.

Peter slumped in his chair and sipped his wine, not meeting my eyes.

Trudie followed me out of the dining room. "Lovely to have you," she said, leaping in front of me to open the front door. "I hope to see you again soon."

I barreled toward the car, feeling murderous. But once the chauffeur pulled out of the driveway, separating me from that toxic house, my thoughts turned to Phoebe, and my anger melted into sorrow. Yes, I would climb into bed when I got home, kiss her if she was awake, read *The Times* with her in the morning. Our life together could continue, whether or not I kept Anthony's cabin. That future, however, would demand a constant suppression. When I believed that Anthony hated me, I could thrive on the subtle attraction I felt for Phoebe. Now, from the grave, he flooded me with a passion I had thought was long extinguished. I hoped I could snuff it out once more, and I hoped I couldn't.

As the car sailed through the darkness, I understood that the price of my inheritance was too steep. I wished Peter had never found me. ◇

The Salt Eater
for Sam

Jane Collins

Its color is snow, hard bite of ice
    but the taste of sea, trapped in glass,
as if a paradise
    was forced to fill a demitasse—
    he reaches for it instinctively, whereas

I, so civilized, refrain and say
    "That's just for putting on your food"
but he must disobey.
    He knows the tang and brackish flood
    in his mouth means more than blind servitude.

He is three and more able to see
    where pleasure sits on a table—
he sees oceans, tiny
    but potent, waiting, unable
    to deluge this world, contained like Babel

Tower's builders, who spoke one language
    until they dared to defy God.

Then, old songs they sang, which
    had always made the crowds applaud,
    made no sense. Or, did they make more? What fraud

do I commit with forbidding? They dared
    and their tongues tasted words unfurled
like sugar ribbon, pared
    off some great spool of sound. This world
    sings with their revolt. And his fingers, curled

around that shaker, feel the quick pulse
    of mutiny beating in piles
of dried-up sea. Why else
    the furtive look, the fox-like guile?
    This small boy, he could lick Lot's wife and smile. ◇

Setting Stone

Jane Collins

The tapping starts at six o'clock—
a music of loose percussive clicks—
my neighbor is rebuilding a wall of rock.
His meditative rhetoric
of long pauses, shrill clinks
then stone-deep silence shrinks
the distances of evening—
I can hear his chisel, reasoning.
What would he think, the long-dead
farmer who harvested those stones
heaved up each spring and spread
on his fields? The earth's unhealed bones
he gathered and tossed into rough rows
that became boundaries through slow
accumulation. He did not mean
to make a wall, only to clean
his land for planting and drop his seeds.
But tonight, I don't hear his hope echo
through my trees. I hear my neighbor, freed
from his office, on his knees, chipping stones
to balance—"one over two,
two over one"—to woo
stones with patience. It is prayer

to take chisel to stone, to pare
or crack them until they fit the waiting
space. Glaciers, racing south
left them here and he, setting
these stones in place, the chinks like mouths
to feed, suspends that race and slows
this night to its moments, and goes
on tapping, tapping as night comes down
until, at last, he leaves off his song. ◇

Cockfight

Sheila R. Lamb

1875: Eastchester, New York

"**B**y God, it's hot." Hugh wiped his brow. Fists up, he was ready to take on Rory Lynch. A sucker punch to the kidney was tempting. A swift upper cut to the jaw would do nicely.

Mosquitoes buzzed around his ears. He'd curse the humidity and the insects but little good it would do him. Dirt dusted up as he kicked at the bare patch of earth. Humid, but no rain. Yet. Clouds pressed down upon him. He kicked at the ground again with the toe of his brogans.

His silhouette was illuminated by the gaslight that escaped through the open door of Spillane's saloon. His chest and shoulders were slick with sweat. He left his suspenders on over his bare torso. No man needed his trousers falling off during a fight.

Rory spat into the darkness. "C'mon, Lamb. What are you waiting for? Can't show up a quarryman?"

Hugh's neck tightened at the insult. A tanner, he made the leather gloves Rory wore while cracking marble. The tannery was dirty work. Vats of urine, fat, and freshly skinned cowhides were what it took to supply the company with work gloves for teams of quarrymen. Rory was dusted white with lime at the end of the day but somehow that was more respectable than curing skins.

Men had followed Hugh and Rory out from the pub, eager for another night's entertainment. Mostly quarrymen, they had cheered for

Rory when the two men pulled off their long-sleeved shirts, preparing for the fight. Hugh's father arrived just as Hugh pushed Rory out the saloon door.

John Lamb nodded his approval. Hugh knew his father heard Rory's taunts every day at the tannery, situated in the work yard of the marble quarry down at the end of Cronin's Road. No man should take the ridicule, his father had told him more than once.

Hugh had held back from fighting Rory Lynch for a reason. He glanced over his shoulder. There he was. James Joy, Mariah's father. Mariah, the woman he wanted to marry. People had taken to calling her Mary. No, *Mar-i-ah*. He thought her name with the proper Irish lilt. It rang through his mind like chimes.

James Joy was a stonecutter, an artisan. He seemed to have risen above the petty woes of laborers. He stepped a slight foot away from the drunken men. His look was blank, as though he neither approved nor disapproved of Hugh's impending actions. The tendons in Hugh's neck stiffened again. He could impress James Joy with the fight. Or not.

Whiskey burned warm in his belly. He had sipped at his glass at the bar while he waited for his Da. The saloon filled up around him. Quarrymen stumbled in first, causing commotion with their heavy boots and loud Irish brogue. The more responsible men went home first and changed out of their lime-dusted clothes, ate supper with their families before a night of drinking. Farmhands trickled in last, only a few willing to walk the distance into Waverly Square.

A group of raucous quarrymen, including Rory, shoved their way up to the bar, pushing Hugh aside. With loud guffaws, they ordered a round of pints. Spillane slammed down wet glasses, sloshing black porter on the oak bar top.

Rory sniffed the air. "What's that smell?"

Hugh stared straight ahead at his own reflection in the mirror behind the bar. Unlike the men who lifted marble, Hugh bathed at home almost daily, an unusual habit. The odor of piss and leather clung to him anyway.

"Who here needs their shirts mended? Lamb here can sew as well as any woman!"

Hugh gritted his teeth so that his jaw ached. It was a stupid slur on his craft. Rory wouldn't dare toss the same words onto Mulchahy, the tailor.

Rory was new to the Masterton Quarry. He had quarried in Manhattan and liked to brag about his time in the city. When the marble sites commenced work again after a seasonal closure, Rory, loud and brash, arrived in a wave of new employees. Few families stuck it out in Eastchester, particularly in the Waverly neighborhood, during the closures. They moved to other quarries, to factories, or back to the borough slums. Hugh and his father were proud of their loyalty to the company.

In the mirror's reflection, Hugh spied James Joy at a back table of the saloon. He sat with another stonecutter and slowly sipped a Jameson. Hugh admired the older man's quiet authority. Quarrymen respected him. He raised his voice only when he gave orders to his men as they loaded tons of refined marble, shaped and smoothed by the artisans, onto railcars.

Hugh decided that he too would drink his whiskey with moderation and control. A sharp contrast with the men around him, whose voices became louder as the drink took hold. A cock crowed from the fighting ring, in a newly built room in the back of the pub. Hugh knew of some men who fought their roosters. Good money if they won their bets. Perhaps he would inquire about raising a rooster himself.

Rory sidled up to him and jabbed an elbow in his ribs.

"Don't touch me, Lynch." Hugh clenched his glass more tightly and wished for his father's presence. John had to take care of Catherine, Hugh's ill mother, first, then knock some sense into the youngest son, William, who constantly threatened to run away and be a railroad man. Family had to be settled before a Saturday night drink.

"Lamb, have you no sense of humor?"

Hugh ignored him.

"You see James Joy back there?" asked Rory. "I have a mind to court his girl. Mary. What do you think of that, Lamb?"

Hugh placed his glass to his lips with careful deliberation. Rory must have seen him talking to Mariah after Mass. The Lamb and Joy families lived on the same street but sat several pews apart in church. Hugh and his father preferred to stay near the open door. Last week, he'd finally gotten up the nerve to ask Mr. Joy's permission to walk Mariah home. He'd spent a month getting his question just right, asking in such a way as to balance confidence and respect.

Mr. Joy had looked to his daughter. Mariah nodded, and then so did he. "Bring her home directly."

The Joy family walked ahead, and his family behind them (Hugh was conscious of William's snickers the entire time). The blue silk ribbon on Mariah's summer straw bonnet matched her eyes. She graced him with a wide smile as he made small talk about the sun and the heat.

Rory'd use anything he could to needle him. Still, the thought of Rory with Mariah made his stomach churn.

Rory jabbed him with his elbow again. Hugh swallowed the last of his whiskey then grabbed Rory by the shirt collar.

"Outside," said Spillane as he continued to pour drinks.

Hugh knew the rules. It wasn't his first fight, but it would be his first with Rory. He unbuttoned his shirt and so did Rory. Neither could afford a damaged collar or a ripped sleeve. He threw his shirt and collar to the ground, then stepped forward and swung wide. His bare knuckles contacted Rory's cheekbone with a solid thwack. Rory returned the punch. His fist missed Hugh's face but knocked him on the side of the head, a hard crack above his ear. Hugh's stance wavered and his vision blurred. He couldn't lose his balance. Not now. Better a broken nose or jaw than have Rory Lynch, a bigger, barrel-shaped man, get him to the ground. Hugh would never be able to push him off. Agility was his strength.

Rory swung again and Hugh ducked. They danced around each other, throwing jabs at the air.

"Don't let him get away with that, Rory!"

"Take down the filthy tanner!"

"Hold steady, son." Hugh's one voice of support. His father's.

Hugh ran his fist upward, delivering a solid uppercut to Rory's jaw. The quarryman quickly rebounded, throwing another left hook. Then he barreled toward Hugh as if to rush him with a tackle. Hugh jumped aside. Rory crashed into the cast-iron hitching post. Stunned in mid-crouch, he keeled over as blood trickled from his forehead.

"What's that about showing up a quarryman?" Hugh glanced around at Rory's comrades. "The rest of you, keep your mouths shut from now on, would you?"

Blood rushed through his arms, his hands. Had one of them caught his eye, he would have fought again. He was ready. He kicked Rory's bare ribcage, leaving a mark of brown dirt from his boot.

"Good, son." His father clapped him on the shoulder. He handed him a flask. Hugh took a long pull of whiskey. From the corner of his eye, he saw James Joy walk past. Nothing from the man. Damn.

"Joy thinks more of himself than he should," his father said.

"I guess he can, Da. He's a stonecutter, a real craftsman."

"Admiring of him, are you? Wasn't long ago when he was hauling rock just like Rory. Jimmy and I came off the same ship. Left out of Cork together. He doesn't need to put on airs."

Hugh wiped his arm across his mouth. Sour whiskey blended with salty sweat. He loved that taste—the taste of a hot summer night and a well-fought victory. Mariah.

Two quarrymen hauled Rory to his feet, where he spat out white tooth chips. The trio stumbled across Waverly Square to the boarding-house. They threw Hugh angry looks, but they'd leave him alone. For now.

"You don't regret it, do you, son? Working in the stink and hides as we do?"

"No, Da. We've got our wages. They couldn't do their job without our gloves. They know it."

Still, he looked down at his hands; brown as the leather he worked. He wondered if Mariah would let his stained hands touch her white skin. ◇

4 A.M.
Black Dog

Pamela Manché Pearce

4 A.M. Black Dog
Stalker
Barks me
Fast into white cold,
Wide awake.

Dripping his acid drool,
Showing teeth, tarred ruins of bone,
He pants hot and steady
With the fetid breath of asses licked clean
And clean again.

4 A.M. Black Dog drags me from my holiday called sleep.
Curled safely, I thought, as I was tight inside my mother
But now I trade her thumping, bloody broth
For dreams, blurred narratives, where
Oceans float giant birds as boats,
Their wings become sails of cobalt, lilac, chartreuse.
And my third-grade teacher, Miss Conduit,
Works in a dry cleaner's shop where

Clothes swing around the racks and turn
To carcasses inside the plastic film.
But she doesn't care—
All dolled-up with pastel flowers in her hair.

Terror skitters across my unconscious:
I'm old and alone with just a walker
And the stink of piss.

4 A.M. Black Dog snarls me to my feet.
Rivulets of sweat, like liquid ice,
Streak the pajamas close-clammed against my skin.
I wait it out.

Day spreads oh, so, so slowly.
A golden ooze across the sky
Shoos away the shadow hound,
A cowering puppy in retreat,
4 A.M. Black Dog now
A mere fleeting spot of remembered dark ◇

Spring on Brite Avenue

Bonnie Jill Emanuel

A mailman says *Hello*
in techniglow, the world
breaks open this day,
pink flowers cry red, yellow, Carolina blue
hashish, a rainbow.
Streets and brilliance
the sky a color
dismembered clouds.
The risks one takes just looking.
The anguish.
The aesthetics.
The Pink Angels by de Kooning.

Other risky days
any of days
the day each child came
became, cried, the husbands
the weeping and blood.
Mornings in libraries
books and walls, explosions

on deaths, possibility.
The day you kissed me.
The red jeans, the red street.
The promise.

The peonies are just shoots
today—red barbs, rhubarb
people eat scrambled eggs
the whites, the neighbors
are gray.
I'm going blind, it hurts
it's beautiful, it's blue and yellow
tearing and lighting up rhubarb stalks
I'm going up in red smoke
brights and hope
the multicolor flowers. ◇

Uncle Henry's Life Lesson

Campbell Geeslin

WHEN SISTER LADY BEATRICE FLOATED INTO A ROOM, EVERY man's watch began to run faster. "Yes," Uncle Henry told me, "that woman appeared to be floating."

This happened back in the days before men wore wristwatches. They had flat little clocks that were kept in special pockets in their trousers. Uncle Henry said, "Sister Lady Beatrice arrived, and I felt as if minnows were swimming around in my gizzard."

Sister Lady Beatrice was welcome at all the summer cottages around the lake in Vermont. After the first greetings, she would suggest a game of dominoes.

Uncle Henry said she was the finest domino player he ever saw. Or did she win just because the men were distracted by their racing pocket watches?

They played winner-take-all and kept score with poker chips. Lady Sister Beatrice stacked them high. After the game, each of the three men at the table would hand Sister Lady Beatrice a five-dollar bill. She would smile, thank them and float out. The screen door shut soundlessly.

Those games went on for years. Then one June day when Sister Lady Beatrice floated in, Aunt Cora told Uncle Henry to get up. She took his place at the domino table. Aunt Cora wasn't wearing a time-piece.

The two women quickly turned the game into a duel. As soon as each player put down a domino, Aunt Cora counted to herself. She then knew every domino that each player had, and she played accord-ingly. From the beginning, Aunt Cora's skill brought in the chips, and she won.

After that, Sister Lady Beatrice never stopped by their cottage again.

Uncle Henry always ended his story with this observation, "That last game taught me something important: all it takes to wipe out the great sensation that grabs a man when a beautiful woman enters a room is another woman who plays a better game of dominoes." ◇

Temporary Wisdom

Susan Prevost

After the storm, we were sad
but we were certain of things.

When a friend denied us sanctuary
in her empty house, we laid her to rest
without tears or ritual in the soft swamp
of memory. When a neighbor provided
food cooked on a green camp stove, we
married her in our hearts.

Surges of truth came from the dark
waters and toppled over us until
we learned its language.

Now, years later, the overcast of doubt
covers everything and I'm the last
to choose sides or call out a sin. ◇

The Garden between the Lucky Hotel and the Moonlight Inn

Sharon Medoff Picard

OUR SECOND MORNING IN SAIGON AND I AM AWAKENED, AGAIN, by the sounds of a baby crying. I sit up in bed and swing my legs over the side, feet groping for slippers. "I'm coming," I whisper, moving on autopilot to get out of bed and check.

The cool of ceramic tiles shocks me into opening my eyes, reminding me of where I am. And that it is only the two of us, Jed and me.

I LOOK DOWN from our room on the fourth floor of the Lucky Hotel. Parting white gauze curtains, I see a garden with close-cropped dry grass and two trees: a large flowering jasmine and an acacia, leaves clustered like slender fingers dipping toward the ground. A curious garden with its mélange of vegetables, solitary flowers, and the odd clutch of chickens. A territorial rooster heralds the morning at five-seventeen.

I don't mention the crying baby to Jed; it will only worry him. In truth, I also brood that he'll respond by making me feel crazy. "Have you been taking your meds, Lucy?" "Do you think we should call Dr. Foley, Lucy?" Easier to keep some things to myself.

When I release the lever to open the window, a drift of hot, humid air settles over my face like a sodden towel, its heavy weight filling my nostrils. The atmosphere brings with it the scents and sounds of Saigon—a fusty pastiche of mildew and diesel oil cut with garden clippings and street food, some of it left out too long. I hear the low grumble of trucks and buses from the nearby main street and the klaxon of motorbikes with the din of insistent honking that marks each biker's effort to navigate the chaos of Saigon's fevered traffic.

Listless, I close the window, letting the curtains drift back over the glass, and I turn to face the room. The furniture is modern and anonymous, with a thick wooden headboard, a beige coverlet embroidered with the logo announcing the hotel's name, and three contrasting rust-colored pillows that sit in stiff attendance at the head of the bed. The name of the hotel seems to be everywhere. Perhaps they are afraid we'll forget where we are. "Lucky Hotel" is even inscribed on the white towels in our room and on the frosted glass doors.

"Lucky Hotel?" I said to Jed when he told me about it.

"I know; I thought the same thing. But, it's in a nice area in the seventh district." Jed's tone was too jovial. "It'll be good for us."

I looked at Jed that day without responding, my answer stuck in my throat. Then I took my iPod from my pocket, put the buds into my ears, and turned Springsteen on at full volume.

WE THOUGHT ABOUT RETURNING to Vietnam for years; friends encouraged us to make the trip. We recalled our Southeast Asia days in the late nineties when we felt ennobled by our common shoestring student budgets. And by the itinerary we constructed that limited us to backpacker motels and street food. Any misstep could send us itching into the night from infested bedrooms or shuddering over the toilet hole in a primitive bathroom. But those experiences were badges we wore proudly, marks of our superiority. And a thin veneer for the unacknowledged envy we felt toward wealthy tourists and expats. "They have no idea what Viet Nam (Cambodia/Laos) is really like," we sneered. What we really meant was that their privilege—in whatever country—left us longing for crisp sheets.

I try now to focus on the cadre of young men and women who work at the desk and around the hotel. When we arrived Nguyen bowed, said a stilted, proud, "Hello, welcome Lucky Hotel," and draped our luggage over his narrow frame. Like most of the people we see here, he is rail thin and has smooth cheeks. His hair is always falling into his right eye and he carries a cigarette tucked into the chest pocket of his short-sleeved shirt.

Each time we speak, the owner, Anh, reminds us that he has visited Santa Barbara. He preens himself on his heavily accented command of English. Such self-congratulatory homage fails to impress us but may carry clout with his monolingual staff.

Periodically the owner calls for Nguyen. Jed and I find it humorous that whenever the young man goes missing, he seems to be across the garden at the Moonlight Inn, smoking his reserved cigarette and drinking coffee in its lobby café. Anh must know where he goes but always treats his employee's disappearance with surprise, never acknowledging that Nguyen is giving business to the competition.

I am most interested in the woman who tends the garden outside our window. I watch her from behind our curtain on the fourth floor as she squats, turning the earth and watering the vegetables with a bucket that she labors to carry from a faucet out of my line of sight. I see that she is angular and thin, her face hidden in the shadows under her conical hat.

I get a better look when we have breakfast on our third morning in Saigon. A downpour has postponed our trip to Black Lady Mountain. We sit in the breakfast room, watching the rain make squiggly tracks on the long windows.

We place orders for egg sandwiches and sip orange juice. The young woman from the garden appears at the window. She wears a frayed green tunic with black pants and holds a basket piled high with large brown eggs. Anh, in response to her tapping, opens the window and takes the basket. She sees me and gives me a thin smile. Her cheekbones are high and smooth.

As she turns to go, I notice that she carries a baby in a red sling across her back. The child's face is barely visible in her swaddling, but I assume from the flash of pink stripes that it is a girl. As the woman trots back to where she came from, she curls her hands over the child's feet where they twine near her waist. My heart starts to pound.

The cries I hear in the night. My hands curve involuntarily, closing to the imagined sensation of the child's toes. I am dizzy as I feel the tickling warmth on my palms and bite my lip. "I wonder if they have a dry place to live."

Jed looks up from his *Lonely Planet* guidebook. "Who?" He rubs his hand across his blond buzz cut.

"That woman, the one who tends the garden. She just brought what I assume are our eggs." I point. "She has a baby."

"Oh, yeah, I noticed her. Lives in that lean-to." Jed gestures across the garden to what appears to be a shed, roughly thrown together. The walls are made of corrugated tin and the roof looks like a piece of plywood covered with plastic. "Cute little guy." Jed's eyes slide briefly over the woman and her baby before returning to the *Lonely Planet*.

"I think it's a girl. I hear her at night . . . it wakes me up."

Jed takes off his glasses, blowing on the lenses and wiping them with the cloth from his glass case. "You could have told me."

"I thought . . . I thought I was imagining it. And that you'd worry."

Jed squints and puts on his glasses, looping the thin wires over his ears. Our silence hangs between us like a border country whose language neither of us can understand.

The eggs, when they arrive, are sunnyside and crisp around the edges. They have bright orange yolks that run when we cut into them with a fork. I eat and watch Jed cut his bread into batons that he dips into the thick liquid and sprinkles with salt. I wonder if the woman will feed her little girl eggs or if they are only for the consumption of hotel guests. My eyes keep wandering back toward the window and across the garden. There is no sign of the child or the mother.

Jed, having polished off eggs and toast, wipes his hands on a paper napkin and returns to the guidebook. He finds the entry for our hiking destination and begins to read aloud. "'The name Black Lady Mountain is derived from the legend of Huong, a young woman who married her true love despite the advances of a wealthy Mandarin. While her husband was away doing military service, she would visit a magical statue of Buddha at the mountain's summit. One day Huong was attacked by kidnappers but, preferring death to dishonor, she threw herself off a cliff. She then reappeared in the visions of a monk who lived on the mountain, and he told her story.'"

Jed continues, mentioning the visual drama of the mountain, a massive green cone that soars from the flatland of Tay Ninh province and overlooks rice fields and jungle. He reads about the cloudy and enigmatic legends associated with this mysterious site, legends that shift and transmogrify according to which side of the boundary the teller is on, Cambodia or Vietnam. I listen to his words but I am thinking of Huong. "She wanted peace."

"What?"

"Huong, that woman in the legend. She was desperate for peace. That's why she jumped."

Jed exhales between opened lips and reaches across the table to take my hand. Worry carves a double crease between his eyebrows. With his other hand he taps out his staccato impatience on the wooden table.

THE RAIN HAS STOPPED. Jed goes out for a run in the late morning. "It's too hot for me," I say, glad to see him go. From our window, I see his loping stride propel him down the road. I take a book from my bag, my hat and sunglasses and a bottle of water and make my way to the garden. There is a seat on the low stone wall under the acacia. The sun is milky and sheds moist rays on the garden. I read, but mostly I am waiting.

Before long, the woman emerges from her home. I stiffen and watch as she bends to her yard tasks, the baby on her back. From time to time, she breaks the rhythm of her work to reach back and pat the child or to jiggle her gently.

Lulled by the drone of the heat, my eyes are half-closed, my book forgotten. I feel cradled by the woman's repetitive motions and imagine the sensation of carrying the baby.

The woman moves in a neat and tidy arc until she arrives near my corner of the garden. I smile and gesture with my book. "I came out to read. The weather is nicer now." I gesture toward the sky.

The woman bows her head.

"Your little girl is lovely." I point to the baby on her back. She smiles tentatively. Then she reaches both her hands back until they are touching the child and speaks to me in rapid-fire Vietnamese. I shrug. "How old is she?" I hold out my hands and extend my fingers, counting style.

The woman seems to understand and holds up four fingers . . . *four months old*. Then she returns to her work and I to my book. I lift my eyes every so often and see the child, head drooping in sleep. I feel as though my breathing synchronizes to hers and I am suspended in time and space, rocked trancelike in an encapsulated moment. When the baby rouses and opens her eyes, I am taken aback that they are Asian eyes, so thoroughly had I wrapped her in my own story.

In the coming days, I find every opportunity to retreat to the garden and watch the mother and child. A dialogue composed of words and gestures develops between us. It is thus that we exchange names and I learn that she is called Zhui and her child Cam. Neither of us understands the other, yet I have myself convinced our communication transcends words.

"What do you do out there, Lucy?" Jed asks.

"I spend time with Zhui and Cam."

"Why? What can you possibly have in common with her? You can't even speak to each other." His words are clipped and terse. "We came here to get away together and you keep finding reasons to go off to be with a stranger." I avoid his eyes and do not answer. His voice seems far away. As though I have turned the volume down on the radio.

THE DAY OF OUR HIKE is sunny and clear. I run a comb through my short hair. I had cut it on impulse, thinking how much easier it would be. At first, I hated the way the curling tendrils settled in layers across my scalp. Then, with a sense of sweet emancipation, I let myself enjoy the unaccustomed ripple of air across my neck and the way my eyes looked bigger when freed from their heavy frame of light brown locks. I associated my new look with my new role.

Now my pixie cap mocks me by accentuating the dark smudges under my eyes.

WE BRING OUR HIKING GEAR downstairs to breakfast. I scan the garden looking for Zhui and Cam. Zhui is picking what might be green beans and dropping them into the same sling where she carried the baby. Bend, pick, drop; bend, pick, drop. So it goes.

Drawn by movement, I spy the child on a blanket next to the lean-to. She is lying on her back and Nguyen, sitting beside her, holds an umbrella over her, protecting her from the sun. Diminutive hands and legs are waving in the air, like the darting of butterflies. I wonder if Nguyen is the father and if they all live together in the hut.

While we wait in the lobby for the car and driver that will take us to Tay Ninh province, Anh busies himself showing off his English. "Where you going?" "You married long time?" Then he asks the inevitable question: "You got kids?" "No good wait long time; get too old." He guffaws with apparent satisfaction at his witticism. I duck outside, agitated and nauseated, leaving Jed to deal with an answer.

THE TRIP TO BLACK LADY MOUNTAIN, about three hours northwest of Saigon, distracts me. I sit by the window watching the landscape shift from densely packed apartment complexes and business districts before transitioning to countryside where water buffalo graze alongside the after-thought factory. Then we move into farming areas, rice paddies where men and women bend over their task in murky water up to their calves.

The road is narrow and, in places, dirt-packed. The pecking order of the road dictates the supremacy of trucks and buses, then cars, and finally the motorbikes. This hierarchy is in inverse proportion to the numbers; bikes far outnumber all other vehicles. Some of the buses are cruisers for tourists but far more numerous are the country coaches, jerry-rigged and antiquated, patched together with rope and duct tape, and spilling over with makeshift luggage, cages of rabbits and chickens, and overstuffed bags of produce. Puffing black exhaust and laboring forward, the buses belch forth passengers at unmarked stops along the road. I watch them and wonder about their lives, admiring what I idealize as a bucolic simplicity.

HOT. I tie a bandanna around my forehead to catch the sweat before it goes into my eyes and replace my billed cap. We are struggling a bit, each absorbed in our trek up Black Lady Mountain. There is the muffled sound of other hikers along the trail and the noise of our own boots as they strike the dry surface of the path.

We wander into the Black Lady Temple, grateful for the shade. It takes a few minutes for my sun-sore eyes to adjust to the dimness. A busy quiet suffuses the space as people stand with their palms joined in prayer, light joss sticks, make offerings of fruit and sweets, or, like us, observe the statuary and tile work.

"So, do we head to the summit?" I look at Jed, who nods and puts on his cap. We proceed single file on the trail rising into the trees.

As the guidebook described, Black Lady Mountain towers over the province of Tay Ninh, rising like an iceberg in the ocean. From our place at the peak, we catch sight of the Cao Dai Great Temple with its four towers, Disneyesque in its pink and yellow painted stucco. Fanned out beyond is an infinity of rice paddies, rubber plantations, corn, and cassava.

"What a view." Jed mops his brow with a Kleenex and points out Cambodia. Then, putting his arm around me, he insists on having our guide take our photo. "New beginning, right, Lucy?" Jed looks into my eyes, seeking an affirmation that I wish I could return.

My mind is on Huong, the Black Lady for whom the mountain is named. Where did she stand as she prepared to jump? What did she think and feel at the moment she chose to plummet over the side? I squint my eyes and picture a slight young woman in a conical hat, slender and erect as bamboo. Her face takes on the contours of Zhui's face, with the melancholy and weariness that seize her youth. I cannot separate the mythical Huong from the young mother who ekes out a living in the garden. I think I know them. I think Zhui knows me. I close my eyes.

We stop to drink from our water bottles. "This was a great idea, wasn't it?" Jed is exuberant. "We should do another hike while we're here." He smiles with a puckish lightness that touches me; I have not seen it in so long. "I've always wanted to get to Cat Tien National Park. What do you think? Is it too far for us to do while we're here?"

I wish I were back in the garden.

ON SUCCESSIVE DAYS, I put away any pretense of reading. First I set my book aside; then I no longer even bring it along. I start to accompany Zhui as she picks beans or weeds the beds. I am clumsy as I try to mimic her neat deft movements but I find the repetitive activity mesmerizing, soothing.

"We, my husband and I, we had a little girl. Her name was Maisie." I begin to confide in Zhui, this woman for whom my words mean nothing.

"Maisie was three months old," I unburden myself. "She died." I start to cry. Startled, Zhui looks at me and tilts her head. "She went to sleep one night and she never woke up. They call it 'crib death.'" I am sobbing and I cannot stop. "I miss her so much." I drop the trowel with which I had been turning the earth under the jasmine tree and grope through my pockets for tissues.

"I miss her so much," I repeat in a whisper. I wrap my arms around my midsection, rocking and trying to hold my broken pieces together.

Zhui stands quietly beside me until my sobs slowly subside. Then she goes into her hut and returns carrying a dragon fruit. Its perfectly smooth skin is deep rosy pink festooned with pale ribbons of green. Zhui bows slightly, deliberately, holding the fruit in both hands, extending it to me.

I watch her while I catch my breath and wipe my eyes. Zhui produces a small knife and carves the dragon fruit, exposing white flesh dotted with tiny black seeds. I accept a slice and we sit in the sunshine eating the sweet fruit, crunching on the seeds. My tissues lie forgotten on the grass.

THIRTEEN YEARS AFTER our first trip to Viet Nam, Jed and I, now in our mid-thirties, finally decided to go back. I patted my then barely rounded belly, thinking it would be the three of us making the long transatlantic trip, luggage jumbled with Pampers and onesies. Our as-yet-unnamed and ungendered baby would be seven months old by then. "It'll be great," friends enthused, eager to make plans to take us to new restaurants and to show us their apartments. And we smiled, keeping our secret to ourselves—for the moment—but enjoying our new status as we tried it on like strangely grown-up clothes for the prom.

After Maisie's death in August, neither of us had the energy to change all those December plans. Our last session together with Dr. Foley only underlined just how trapped we were in our respective isolation, blundering about, bruised and incomplete. To discuss what we had lost was a topic too highly charged and painful for our words to take us where we needed to go.

"Enough, Lucy, you have to stop dwelling on it! I can't talk anymore," Jed said, slicing his hand through the air, closing the door I needed to pass through to find him again.

"And you think if we don't talk about it we won't think about it. What a pair we make, Jed. You can't talk about it and I can't talk about anything else." One thing I don't talk about is my dream, the dream I have had with disturbing regularity since the day Maisie died.

I'm on the bed with maisie and I roll over on her when I wake up she's not breathing I start mouth to mouth respiration and jed comes in shouting at me to stop let her go he says she has to go I grab maisie and run leaving jed behind

SITTING IN THE TWILIGHT that evening on the patio of the Moonlight Inn, we make desultory conversation about our hike, about friends, about our dinner choices.

Jed takes my hands. "Aren't you glad we decided to do this, Lucy? We really needed to get away." He rubs my hands gently with his thumbs. "I know it's been hard, but I know we'll get through it." He sounds strong and sure. "Right, Luce?" I look down and sip from my glass of water.

We order marinated beef on lemongrass skewers and summer rolls, delicate skins of rice paper wrapped around cellophane noodles with shrimp, grated radish, and cilantro. We dip them in fish sauce flavored with lime, sugar, and hot peppers while we cool the heat with Tiger beer.

The low hum of voices is cloaked in the falling dusk and seems to muffle any intrusion of traffic sounds from nearby thoroughfares. Suddenly, we are disturbed by an altercation at the corner of the café near the garden. An angry diner explodes in a German accent and calls the maitre d'.

"What's going on?" My back is to the table where the commotion began.

"Woman's trying to sell a lottery ticket or something. The guy's pissed his dinner was disturbed by a huckster."

"All you have to do is say no." I crane my neck to see.

Jed shrugs. "It's annoying. Who wants their dinner disturbed?"

The maitre d' is smiling placatingly at the diner and glowers at the woman as he leads her to the gate. He has her arm in a grip and I see her shake herself free. I catch a glimpse of her face. She is flushed and shaking. Our eyes meet for an instant.

"Oh, my God, Jed, it's Zhui." As she turns to leave I see the flash of red that is the sling for her baby. The child wears a yellow sweater. I glimpse her delicate, beautiful face with its sweet half smile and dark eyes. "How humiliating for her."

"Let it go, Lucy." Jed's voice is expressionless.

"I have to go to her. How awful to be treated like that."

"This makes no sense, Lucy." Jed's voice is barely a whisper. "You can't find Maisie in this woman's child."

I snatch my hands from his and don't try to contain my fury. "I miss her, Jed! I miss her and I need to talk about her. You act as though our daughter never existed!" I am making stabbing motions with my chopsticks. "I don't want to act as though her life didn't matter."

"I'm not acting as though her life didn't matter." Jed removes his glasses and begins to wipe them with his napkin. "I don't think I honor Maisie's life by obsessing about it."

"Jed, I've gotten more sensitivity from a woman who can't understand a word I say than I have from you." I push my chair back with a clatter. "I'm going up to the room."

The sky has darkened and lanterns spread thin ovals of light on the garden. As I walk across to the Lucky Hotel, I see a still shadow near the stone wall.

"Zhui?" My voice is tentative in my ears. She lifts her chin at my greeting. I can see her face clearly, her eyes a cold glitter in the dimness. For a brief moment we are suspended together in the hush of the Saigon night.

Her last gesture to me is a resigned wave of her arm before she places both hands possessively on Cam's legs and trots off into the blackness. The heavy spice of jasmine saturates the night. It follows me as I walk, taunting me with its perfume.

Lump in my throat, I find my way to our room and begin to pack. ◇

Around the World in Nothing Flat

Peggy Aylsworth

Yes, we do have much in common,
but custom wears a coat of many colors.
The hostess in a Thai café we frequent
offered me a lavish compliment.
Touched, I reached out, stroked her arm.
She flinched. Her reflex blunts the gesture.
I swim in the gulf between.

Russians, I've been told, prefer
a conversation in your face,
unlike Americans, who guard their space.
In a French café her story stirs my coffee.
Her Italian lover in Japan had left
a parting message on the phone:
"I hope you come in Italy sometime."

We spin the differences
to bombs, to planes that shatter towers,
bodies feeding a piece of dirt.
The heart breaks open, but in
the new moon's light, who can
see the shadowed whole? ◇

The Lost Flock

Peggy Aylsworth

Pity the poor grebe. Along with its flock,
it plunged to sudden death, as man-
   made
   blacktop
was mistaken, under stormy clouds,
for welcoming waters. Who's to blame?
   Nature
   gave them
feet without mobility on land. Those
who survived were stranded, out of their
   element.
   No parachute,
no compass, relying on instinctive
memory, the betrayal took a holocaustal
   toll.
   We all
live in a deceptive forest, believing
the path well-marked with crumbs.
   How little
   we account
for stealthy wind, a covering of leaves as
we make our way, one foot stumbling on another. ◇

The Old Man and the C

Donald Capone

S ANTIAGO WAS AN OLD MAN, A PICKPOCKET, WHO WORKED ALONE on the C line. He had gone forty-two days now without taking a wallet. The first twenty days he had a boy with him, a scout, who'd move ahead in the subway cars and locate potential victims, or "fish," as the old man liked to call them.

But the boy had since moved on to greener and more lucrative pastures: stealing GPS units from parked cars. Santiago knew his ways were antiquated. People had knapsacks now, or shoulder bags worn across their fronts, everything zipped up tight. It was too late for him to learn a new trade.

Santiago saw the boy getting off the subway at 110th Street. The boy was happy to see him. "Santiago, I can help you again, if you want. I've made some money."

"Don't worry," the old man told the boy. "I'm good. I feel my luck changing. The big fish is out there. Stay with what you're doing."

"Okay," the boy said. "But let me buy you a Starbucks at least."

"Why not?" the old man said. "Between thieves."

They walked up to the Starbucks on 111th Street and Broadway. The boy went to get the drinks while the old man found a table in back, kicked off his shoes, and waited for the boy to return. A newspaper was on the next chair, and Santiago opened it to the sports section.

"How are the Yankees doing?" the boy asked, handing a coffee to the old man. "I'm afraid of the Red Sox this year."

"Have faith, Manny. Think of the great Jeter. He makes the difference."

The boy and the man sipped the coffee silently for a while. Then the boy said, "Are you hungry? I can get us some *tamales*."

"No, I will eat at home," the old man lied.

"Then I should go home and eat with my family."

After the boy left, the old man walked east. He had a good new place under the Metro-North elevated tracks on Park Avenue where he liked to sleep. These days he didn't need much rest, anyway. Plus the early morning trains would wake him from his dreams of lions in the Bronx Zoo. He hadn't been there since he was a kid. Maybe one day he'd make it back before he died, see the lions again. Those beautiful, noble, proud beasts. Though caged, he felt, they were more free than he was.

The next morning at first light, Santiago roused himself from his bed of newspapers in his cardboard shack, and with the last of his money bought a cup of coffee and a bagel from the diner on 116th Street. He knew it would probably be the only thing he ate all day. It would be easier for him to work the 6 line on the East Side, but his face was too well known there, so he had to go way over to the West Side to work the C line. So he began the trek to the subway station at 125th Street and Saint Nicholas Avenue, a good long walk that would get his blood pumping and fully wake him up. He liked to enter the subway as far uptown as possible, so he could watch all the commuters as they got on, scope them out, then move in for the kill when the car got more crowded as it got closer to Midtown. He descended into the station and used the remaining money on his MetroCard to join the current of commuters flowing onto the platform.

A good number of people entered the car at Eighty-sixth Street. Seventy-second Street saw even more squeeze on. By Fifty-ninth Street, everyone was packed in tight. In the old days, this is when it would be easy. The wallets would practically jump into your hand, as people were jostled by the swaying of the subway car and the jockeying for position of the other riders. But those days were long gone. Still, Santiago kept an eye out for the big fish, the one fat belly of a wallet that would sustain him for a good month.

Sometimes Santiago felt he should not have been a thief. Seeing the commuters rushing off to work, meat on their bones, good clothes, a home to return to at night—not to mention a husband, wife, children—made him feel that he should have done something else with his life. But he was a born thief. He couldn't change that. Still, no one should be alone in his old age. And he was alone. He wished the boy was with him.

At each stop, as people exited and entered, Santiago worked his way slowly through the cars, always on the lookout for his big fish. After the Thirty-fourth Street/Penn Station stop, when the crowd thinned, he knew his best chances were through for now. He'd ride down to Fourteenth Street and switch to an uptown train, try to get the commuters coming in from Brooklyn and lower Manhattan. So for now, he grabbed a seat and sat back, waited, felt the subway pull him out toward the end of the island.

Just as Santiago was resting his eyes, the big fish showed himself. He got on at Twenty-third Street, walked past Santiago, and stood in front of the subway map mounted inside the car, studying the route. He was middle-aged, slightly overweight, and had a long nose. He wore an aqua-colored workout suit with purple stripes down the sleeves and legs, and an out-of-fashion fanny pack bursting with maps and papers— and a very worn and very full wallet.

Santiago perked up immediately, flexed his left hand, which had begun to fall asleep. *Don't crap out on me now, hand, I need you,* he thought. The man traced the subway's path with a finger. So much for switching at Fourteenth Street. It looked as if Santiago was going way out to Brooklyn.

Then the man began to move, walking back down the length of the car. Santiago stood and followed. The man reached the end of the car and opened the door and entered the next car. Santiago, keeping a good distance between him and the man, did the same. His eyes were on the man's wallet. The man kept walking. *It takes the both of us,* Santiago thought. *We're in this together. Brothers.*

At the Fourteenth Street stop, the man paused and looked at the subway map again. When the train started to move, the man began to walk once more, through the doors into the next car. Santiago never let him out of his line of vision. He flexed his fingers again, in preparation for the moment, for when he would need them. They had never let him down before, and there was no reason to think that they would now.

The man and Santiago went on in this manner through the remaining Manhattan stops. When the subway crossed under the river into Brooklyn, Santiago knew he was out beyond his usual limits. How far would the man go? He had no choice now but to follow him. Follow in his wake.

There were not enough people in the cars for Santiago to feel comfortable closing the gap as he trailed his big fish into the final car. He held back, hoping the man would tire himself out and decide to sit. Then Santiago would stand next to him, reach in and grab the wallet as the man stood to exit. By the time the man realized his wallet was gone, and fathomed what had occurred, Santiago would be at the next stop, at least.

And that is exactly what happened. Santiago stood next to the man and waited for the train to make its next stop, or the one after, or the one after. Whenever the man decided to get off. Santiago thought again of being a thief. He had no regrets. He was born to be a thief just as the victim was born to be a victim. He wished the boy were here, he'd be proud of the old man.

At the Borough Hall station in Brooklyn, the man hoisted himself up and stood holding the pole, waiting to exit. Standing so close to him, Santiago saw for the first time how big the man was. But Santiago was smarter, or luckier, at least on this day. The car stopped, the doors slid open, and in one quick motion Santiago reached into the fanny pack, removed the wallet, and tucked it into his own front pocket.

Santiago began to move away from the doors to the other end of the car. When the doors closed and the train began to move, Santiago saw the man on the platform, waiting his turn to exit through the turnstile. Santiago felt for the wallet, pulled it from his pocket, and removed the cash and put it in his other pocket. He'd dump the wallet later, and count the cash when it was safe. At the next stop, he'd get off and cross over to head back to Manhattan. It was a long way back. He didn't like to go out this far, but the fish showed himself, and he needed to break his streak of forty-two unsuccessful days.

At Hoyt Street, he got off the train and walked toward the steps to cross over to the Manhattan-bound side. A man stepped off with him, and followed two paces behind. Not unusual, but Santiago was always alert to the ebb and flow of a subway crowd. When he reached the other platform, he glanced over his shoulder. The man was still right behind him. Santiago got a good look at him this time, and knew the look well. Determined, cold-hearted, hungry. Relentless. Had the man seen Santiago with his big fish? Maybe. Santiago would have to prepare for a fight. He thought of the fierce lions as inspiration. He was an old man, but he was experienced. He knew where to hit.

The train arrived and Santiago got on, followed by the man. There weren't many people in this car, so Santiago continued through, hoping the next car would be more crowded. Without looking, Santiago began to disperse the money to each of his four pockets; in case he was robbed he wanted to hold on to as much as he could. The attack came just as he reached the door between the cars. He was hit hard from behind, and felt the man's hands on him, his sharp nails like teeth as they searched for the money. The probing fingers fished out the bills from one pocket just before Santiago threw an elbow that landed on the man's ribs. Santiago opened the door and went through.

There were more people in this car, but what did it matter? No one would help. Santiago was hit from behind again and felt his feet nearly leave the ground. He recovered his balance without falling, but the man hit him hard in the face with his fist. Then a hand in another pocket, and a fist to the back of the head. Santiago had two pockets of money left, which could still be a good amount, if only he could make it home. As the speeding train braked, and the riders swayed, Santiago was thrown to the ground. A kick hit him in the teeth, a boot held down his neck. A third pocket was emptied, and when the doors slid open back at Borough Hall, the man was gone, quickly lost amid the incoming tide of commuters.

With blood in his mouth, Santiago crawled to a corner of the subway car and pulled himself up. He spread out over the last three seats and lay with his back to the wall. The subway car swayed like a boat, and strange thoughts came to the old man's head. He was young again, and approaching a shoreline, where the lions from the Bronx Zoo were pacing back and forth on the sand, as if awaiting his arrival. The boy was there to help him off the boat.

The train crossed over into Manhattan while the old man dozed. He was so tired. He must stay awake, though, so he wouldn't miss his stop. After the train passed Midtown, the station stops began to enter his consciousness. Seventy-second Street, Eighty-first, Eighty-sixth, Ninety-sixth, 103rd, then finally his stop, 110th Street. He rolled off of the seats and stood, bleary-eyed from both the sleep and the swelling to his eyes where he had been punched.

He stumbled off the subway car, and made it up the stairs slowly, his eyes assaulted by the sunlight when he reached the top. He balanced himself against the rail. Then he remembered the money, and his hand found its way to his pocket, the one the mugger had missed. He pulled out the wallet, which he hadn't managed to discard. Looking inside, he saw it was empty. Then he felt himself going down.

"Santiago, Santiago!" It was the boy, grabbing him, holding him up, wrapping an arm around him. "What happened to you?"

"He beat me, Manny," the old man said.

"Not your big fish?"

"No. After. The fish I got," Santiago said. "What did you get today?"

"Four," the boy said. "Four GPS units."

"Very good."

"Forget about me. Here, drink this," the boy said, and handed the old man a bottle of water. Santiago drank, then the boy helped him walk over to a bench just outside Central Park.

"Stay here," the boy said. "I will get you food."

The boy ran off, and the old man slumped over on the bench.

When the boy returned, the old man was asleep. The boy removed his sweatshirt, rolled it up, and placed it gently under the old man's head, then sat next to him.

Santiago was having the lions dream again. He was getting out of his boat, pulling it up to shore; he was young and strong once more. The lions waited for him. ◇

Father Rock Says Mass Barefoot

Pete Reilly

Father Rock said my father's funeral Mass barefoot.

He had pastored a church
scratched from the bleeding side
of an Appalachian slope mine;
the skeleton of an excavator
rusting in the corner
of the gravel parking lot;
a fine black coal dust
coating the empty pews.

Father Rock,
ever the shepherd
in search of lost sheep,
walked the red dirt path
that twisted up the mountain
at the edge of town,
to the broken trailer
that spilled its contents
into the overgrown yard.

Three earnest beagles
announced his arrival,
and being a big man,
his shadow shrouded
the stick-thin woman,
who greeted him,
her face squeezed tight,
defeated,
a battered fist,
that surveyed the world
through a veil of cigarette smoke.

She was barefoot,
her feet callused,
her heart scarred
like the weathered truck tires
littering her lawn;
but he led her down the mountain
to the empty church,
and kicked his own shoes
to the weeds
as he walked,
so she would feel no shame
on entering. ◇

Daddy

Richard Quigley

Dull and discolored, the mirror hangs above my head,
but delicate; the silver backing seems to fracture

each time I gaze at this muted reflection. I yearn
to cope with what is now petrified

by a tarnished slab of splintered wood
once at my father's home near the ocean,

without any trace of flaking. I see him in my blurred
image, his gentle face stained into the glass.

I strive to sense the way he saw himself
on some forgotten July night, closing my

eyes to taste the cradled saline breath that
sticks to the firmness of his adolescent skin.

The imperfect ochre frame as our halo, binding
his ghost, my body.

They stare at one another, longing for answers
we will never have the privilege of knowing. ◇

The Tintype, 1891

Elizabeth L. Gould

T HE SUNDAY BEFORE ALICE AND HER FOLKS QUIT CENTER, TEXAS, for good, Edgar had worked himself up to a swivet. He needed something to remember Alice by, but nothing had presented itself. He'd ridden by her house a week earlier, but a billy goat had taken a dislike to his horse and they'd been driven off the property.

She'd fallen asleep two nights before when babysitting his little sisters for the last time, but just as Edgar had been about to snip a lock of her hair, one of the twins had woken up with a nightmare and startled Alice awake. Edgar had jumped so high, he'd been clear across the room by the time her eyes opened.

His brother, Major, jabbed an elbow in his side as he got out of the bed they shared with Carl, who was already dressed and downstairs. "Move, lard brain." He lay there in bed, ignoring Maj. *Think, dammit!* Maybe Maj was right about what was going on between his ear pans. Even if he pretended to be sick, there was that damn billy goat. He felt awful.

Kitty stuck her bossy four-year-old nose in his business again, leaning into his room from the safety of the doorway. "Edgar! Momma says quit lollygagging!"

He rolled over, away from her, ignoring the urge to yank the bow from her hair and lay waste to it. "I'm sick. Buzz off, Maggot." So what if he'd worked himself up to it? He could feel his guts churning. His head was riled up to match.

His mother, Octavia, clucked her way into the room, a frown on her face that disappeared when she laid a hand on his forehead. "Pumpkin, you've got a fever!"

And so, as the rest of the poor bastards drove off to church that morning, Edgar found himself with three hours on his hands, free to do as he pleased. It went without saying he wasn't going to be following his mother's dictates to stay in bed.

Edgar snuck into the paddock and made off with the fastest horse he dared to ride bareback. Acorn was frisky with nothing but a halter on, but he hadn't wanted to risk being seen by one of the cowboys. He slowed down by the edge of Alice's property and tethered Acorn to a tree. The house and grounds were quiet as midnight. They'd penned the billy goat in the corral over by the barn, too. Damned if the old goat wasn't looking straight at Edgar, bleating its heart out.

Edgar smiled. "No one can hear you, you dumb goat." He tried the back door. Open. He walked on in, calling out, "Hello?" No answer. The help was still off at church, too, then.

The draperies blocked most of the available light. Large trunks were laid out in the open areas, most of them filled with folderol. Crates took up what little space was left. He squeezed between two trunks and a dark-green Victorian high-back sofa and walked upstairs.

It wasn't hard to find Alice's bedroom, seeing as how she was the only girl in the family. It was pink, floor to ceiling. Clothes spilled over the tops of two trunks. His lip curled on its own. How in hell could he find a keepsake in all this wretched pink? He stuck a hand out to balance as he passed the vanity. Glass vials crashed to the floor. He bent to scoop them up, cutting his fingertips. "Damn!" He stood up again. And then he saw it: a tintype of Alice. Perfect.

He snatched it up and ran. He made it back in time to turn the horse out into the paddock, put the tintype in his cubby hidey-hole, and get back in bed.

Not half an hour later, in walked his momma. "How's my pecan pie?" She kissed his forehead. "Still hot and sweaty, you poor thing."

She smoothed his hair back and glanced down at the sheets. "My stars and garters! What on earth happened here?"

Edgar's heart sank as he followed her gaze to the blood on the sheets; on his fingers as she pulled his hands out from under the covers. "I cut myself, Momma."

"While you were home sick in bed?" She touched the oozing tips.

His father, Daniel, walked in. "I checked on the horses and Acorn's all lathered up. Would you know anything about that, son?"

Octavia held Edgar's hands out for Daniel to see. Edgar looked from his father to his momma and back again, all the words in the world stuck in his tongue, just as his tongue was stuck to the roof of his mouth. Might as well have been frozen, for all the use it was. His eyes, saucer-wide, admitted his guilt as his tongue never would.

Daniel started removing his belt. "God as my witness, on your deathbed we'll be dragging you to church! See if you ever stay home again in your life!"

Octavia put a hand on Daniel's arm. "Remember the age rule, now, Daniel."

Daniel took a deep breath. "How old is he again?" With eleven children, he'd long forgiven himself for losing track.

"Twelve."

Edgar thought of the tintype of Alice, snugged away in his cubby. It was worth it. ◇

I'll Miss You

Maryann Stafford

I'll miss you

when summertime heat
calls me to an upstate waterfall
and the drop is farther down
than I remembered

When Christmas crackers explode
turning to crowns and cheap trinkets
the mincemeat pies
and your mother's door-stopping pud

How you loved Christmas and waterfalls and me
but the drop was farther down than we knew
and The Ghost of Christmas Future refuses
to wear his silly paper crown ◇

Paper Wings

Maryann Stafford

There's more to life than people
As a Catholic girl groomed toward self-abandonment
a seedling in the shade growing sideways
aiming for a shiny bit of mica in the wall
instead of the sun
I was bent

The slant is to please, help, comfort,
sacrifice for others
as you place your head under the wheel
but there's more to life than people

There are exuberant winds on hilltops
where a butterfly's paper wings
face into the oncoming wave and never buckle

There are clover, sticky pinecones,
twitching tails of squirrel in the pink dogwood
and tiny purple flowers among the low-lying weeds
near my unsandaled foot

By the undemanding junipers there is only breath
soft and easy

A centipede ambling over a paving stone reminds
that repulsion has many legs
acceptable or no

You have taken enough of me
dear ones, family, church
Your false flickering light no longer tricks
the eye or dictates direction

Because there's more to life than people
In this found field of contentment ◇

Ashland Man

Dylan Gilbert

COWS: DUMPSTER-SIZED LUMPS, PELT-COVERED, THICK HEADS WITH *gentle faces, legs tucked under their mass. Silent, still, clustered under an ancient sycamore whose craggy arms reached outward, embracing the lunky creatures in shade. The dirty-white, the only one standing, frozen like a museum. The silky-brown just outside the shade, her dirt-red fur catching yellow rays of sun. The baby brown, curled in a ball, resting against the hillside of her mother.*

The dirty-white bent her front legs, her body trembling and straining as she lowered her chest to the ground. She repeated this action with her hind legs and she too became a legless hulk. The silky-brown in the sun chewed her cud, as did the black-and-white just ahead of her in the shade. There they lay, the nine of them, as if they had been dropped, giant and legless, from the sycamore. Content to just be, like a hill or a barn.

THE OLD MAN WAS A FARMER, one of the last in Ashland, with a yard full of hens and nine cows. He was tall and gangly, with a gray beard and stiff knee. He had had friends here in the past: Morton, Tolliver, Buckley. Only vague images and thoughts now. He used to get calls from Tolliver after he moved away, but that stopped two years ago. Maybe four.

He didn't talk to people much anymore—now and then to that couple next door with the naked children and the guitar playing. They brought him flowers when his wife died, invited him to dinner, where he politely ate a strange meatless stew. The husband sometimes asked him for tools, but he hadn't seen him for some time now. He used to chat with the tourists he rented rooms to for the festival. They were polite, refined, interested in him and the area, but he was always relieved to see them go, to turn off the show, to put on his patched jeans and smelly T-shirt and crack open a beer. He hadn't rented to them for months now, maybe a year.

Though he had never made an attempt to keep up with his old friends from town, though he never felt he'd had a particularly success-ful marriage or was especially close with his only child, a daughter who had moved to Los Angeles over 30 years ago, there were times, like on a Saturday evening with the TV on or a Sunday walk through his town of strangers, when he missed the presence of family and friends. Some he hadn't seen in years or even decades, yet now felt the loss of them.

The loneliness twisted him at times, weakened him. Some days he forced himself to plow through it, but more often it leeched his energy and drive. At times he pretended it didn't exist, but it was always lurk-ing. He pictured ways of escaping it, with gas from the stove or a bullet from his old Winchester.

THE COWS HAD BEEN TAKEN THAT MORNING. The fellow with the long curly hair and freckles had given him the check two days before, but he hadn't deposited it yet. Wasn't so much—he practically gave them away. But they'd be on a good piece of land, better than his, more space at least. The fellow kept grinning and shaking his hand, this lightness in his eyes over nine old cows. He had to help the guys load them into the cattle carrier they had rented, saw they didn't know cows. They'd have spent the day there if the old man hadn't shoved a dripping hand of molasses toward the lead brown's nostrils and brought her into the trailer.

The patch of land under the sycamore was clear now, the hulks lying there for the past 50 years gone. He peeked out a few times and flinched when he saw the empty space. But then remembered and the remembrance caused a thorny feeling in his belly. He stepped out, walked to the sycamore, saw the flattened grass where the cows had been. Why had he let them go? he wondered. But then the worry drifted away, replaced by the desire to close things out in his life. Too much responsibility, those cows. He wanted his affairs cleaned up.

He shifted on the couch so the springs close to the surface didn't jab at his legs and buttocks. He took another sip of his half-full Schlitz and his eyes wandered back to the TV, where some young cops were investigating a crime scene, but he had no clue what the show was about. He gazed out at the cowless fields again.

He heard a wailing. A common sound, the neighbor's kids, all the time hooting, hollering, and carrying on. The children lived almost like feral animals, playing in the dirt and weeds all day, even at night, half dressed, unkempt. It had gotten worse since the father left.

There it was again, the wailing, more shrill this time. Can't this lady care for her young ones? he thought. She's nice enough, but irresponsible. He knew the difficulty of having to fend for yourself at a young age. He had been one of seven kids. His mother had died the day after birthing the eighth, a stillborn. From then on, he and his younger siblings survived mostly on their own, his father and older brothers working long hours, six days a week. He left his warm beer and stepped out on his porch.

The neighbor boy was sprawled in the gravel beside a bike, moaning softly. The old man was irritated. How come this woman doesn't mind her children? He limped to the boy and stood over him. "You all right, boy?"

The child whimpered and looked at his injured leg. The old man saw the knee, skin scraped off and caked with gravel. The foot had a gash that trickled blood. "I'll get your mom."

"She's not home," said the boy.

The old man peered down at him, the problem of the hurt boy taking on more weight now. I'm not responsible for this child, he thought, starting to twist himself up in barbwire and resentment, thinking to walk away and leave the child there. The boy had pale skin and long, lank hair that hung in his eyes. He was biting into his lower lip, fighting the pain. The old man reached a big leathery hand to the boy and pulled him to his feet. He clung to the old man's fingers as they walked to the steps of the boy's house.

"Where's your mom?"

"Work," he said through gritted teeth.

The man grunted. They stood, the boy grimacing, the man squinting toward the road, hoping for the mom to show. "Guess we better clean that up. Come on."

He took the boy into the house. Colorful tapestries lined several walls, faded Oriental rugs covered the floors. He led the boy to the bathroom, eased off his sandal, and began to wash his bloody foot in the tub. "Next time you should wear shoes."

The boy looked at him with curious eyes, dust on his brow and long, blond-white hair. "I did," he said, pointing to his flimsy rubber flip-flops, now on the bathroom floor.

"No, shoes like these," said the old man, pointing to his hiking sneakers. "Don't you have some tennis shoes to play in?"

The boy shook his head.

After finishing the boy's foot, the old man tried to clean his knee with a wet washcloth, but the boy screamed and squirmed away. "All right, all right," said the old man. That dirt's not going to hurt him anyway, he thought. Leave it be.

There were no bandages in the medicine cabinet, just cough syrup, a box of tampons, and a few jars of herbs. The old man told the boy to wait and went back to his place. He found a mildewed box of Band-Aids in his medicine cabinet and brought them back to the boy.

He bandaged the boy's foot and his dirt-caked knee as best he could and left him in front of the TV. He picked up the bike, looped the chain back on, and left it on the porch next to some empty rabbit cages.

When he got home, he thought to tell someone about the neglected boy riding with no shoes that he had helped, but couldn't think of anyone to speak to. His friends up the road that he used to talk with had been gone for years. He thought to call his daughter, but realized she probably wouldn't listen. She'd tell him he shouldn't have helped the boy for fear of being sued or some such nonsense. He sat, words and images from the TV flowing into the back of his mind, took a swallow of warm beer.

The next day the mother and the boy and the wee girl came with a handful of wildflowers and a hand-drawn card with pictures of animals and backward letters. The mother was grateful and thanked the man over and over again, standing in the doorway, clasping one of his big hands in hers. The old man, his belly tense, nose crinkled, looked down at his feet and said he had hardly done a thing and they were making too big a fuss. He eased his hand out of hers and mumbled goodbye as he shut the door.

When they were gone, he dug up one of June's old vases from the closet and set the flowers and card on the TV.

ASHLAND: *Wheat-colored hills and snow-crowned mountains in the distance. Houses, unkempt and colorful: Tibetan flags, Buddha statues, Zen gardens, piles of bicycles, kayaks, and furniture splayed out on porches. Wildflowers, tall and weedy, in glorious clumps: yellow bell, lupine, chicory.*

Clusters of boys on road bikes coming from the hills; pony-tailed men driving Priuses and old diesel Mercedes; free-spirited skateboarders; hippies, tanned and smiling, in loose hemp clothing; elderly tourists, wearing L.L.Bean and Lands' End, on their way to the Shakespeare Festival; groups of young, dreadlocked white men, tattooed and musty, with cardboard signs begging for money.

THE OLD MAN RARELY LEFT THE HOUSE. He used to go to the farmers' market twice a week to sell milk and the few eggs the old hens still produced, but that ended once he sold the cows. He used to have friends he would run into in town or visit at their homes, but there was no one left to see. His acquaintances had drifted away once the mills began closing, and even more so after his wife died. Some days he forced himself out. He made himself take a bath and run a comb through his hair. Then he would make his way to town.

On the walk that morning, he stopped in front of Tolliver's old house, a brown bungalow on a half-acre or so. He thought about times when he and June had sat on that porch with Tolliver and Val, sipping beers and enjoying the hot summer nights. He had an urge to knock on the door and ask the owners if they knew where Tolliver was now, but was discouraged by the two large mutts sleeping on the porch and a front yard filled with dry dog shit.

In town, thinking of the boy with the cut foot, no shoes, and no minding, he walked into the sporting goods store. All the sneakers looked a bit obscene to him, strange orange and green and black patterns, shiny and space-like. He settled on a pair that looked to be about the right size, white with black stripes, the only ones that looked like shoes to him. As the clerk was ringing up the shoes, the old man told him to throw in a pack of boys' tube socks.

When he returned he found the boy behind his house, shoeless, his bandages filthy, throwing rocks in the pond, which was now more of a mud puddle. The old man limped to him and the boy smiled. He handed him the shoebox and the bag of socks. "Next time you ride, wear these."

A few minutes later, in his kitchen, heating up a can of ravioli, he heard the rattle of a bike outside. He stepped to the window and pulled the curtain to the side. The boy rode around in big circles on the field of dead grass that separated their two houses. He looked at the boy's feet, but couldn't see if he had shoes on. He squinted when the boy's arc took him closer, but all was a blur as he zipped by.

He put on his hat and stepped out and walked to the boy's yard. The boy rode up to him, and they watched each other in silence, the white-hot sun breathing down on them. The old man glanced at the shoes on the boy's feet. "How do they fit?"

"Good."

Something had grabbed his attention and he looked down at the shoes again. The laces dangled below the pedals. "Why, you've got to tie those."

The boy looked down at the laces but said nothing.

"Those'll get caught in the gears, and you'll fly right over the handlebars."

The boy looked at the old man and shrugged.

"Why don't you tie them?" said the man.

"I can't."

He studied the child, unsure of his meaning. "Why not?"

"Don't know how."

The old man furrowed his brow. He'd never heard of a boy this age—he must be eight or so—not tying his own shoes. Then he sighed. "All right." He started edging his way down to a knee, and for a moment it seemed as if he'd lose his balance till he got a hand on the ground to steady himself. He pulled a lace on his own shoe to untie it. With the laces loose now, he made a loop with his shaky left hand, then another with the right, which was quicker and smoother. The boy leaned forward over his handlebars, watching closely. The old man tied the loops in a clumsy knot creating a bow. "Give it a try."

The boy laid the bike down and sat on the ground. He wrestled with his laces till he got them both looped, but when he attempted to knot the two, it all turned to spaghetti. He looked to the old man. "All right, come over here." The boy stepped to the old man, who had lowered himself to his seat. He reached out to the boy's closer foot and looped each lace with his big fingers. "See, loop, loop, then tie the loops in a knot." The old man looked up at the boy, the sun glaring in his eyes. "Got it?"

The boy nodded. The old man pulled the string, releasing the bow. "Go ahead now." The boy sat on the ground in front of the old man, focused all his attention on the laces, and started the loops.

Sitting in the dead grass and dust, the boy got both shoes tied.

"Now you're ready to ride," said the man. The boy smirked, walked to the bike, and hauled it up. He climbed on and began making bold circles in the field.

The old man got to his feet and stood, watching. When the boy passed him, he'd sit up a bit and once he yelled, "They fit gooder now."

The man nodded, a smile edging into his eyes.

He trudged back to his house and up the stairs. "Bye," called the boy from his bike. The old man lifted a hand.

THAT NIGHT the old man heard a knock on the door. He set his can of Schlitz on the side table and pushed himself out of the chair. "Coming." Probably someone who wants my damn money, he thought.

He pulled the squeaky door open and there stood the boy's mother, wearing a long dress and a generous smile. She hugged him. "Thank you for being so sweet to Matthew," she said, holding the old man in her arms. He stiffened, mumbled it was nothing. The softness of her body reminded him of June, how she would wrap her arms around his neck, lean into him, and lay her cheek on his shoulder, and that hug would pull some of the poison out of the day. He felt a tightness in his chest, a warmth and sadness. He cleared his throat several times and backed away from her. "Well, again, I just want you to know how much it means to me, you helping Matthew and all. He's crazy about you."

"Is that right?"

She nodded, smiling up at him.

The old man grunted. "Haven't seen your husband lately."

He thought he saw a flash of darkness in her face, but then it was gone. "He's been away."

"Oh. Be back soon?"

She smiled, her teeth clenched. "I don't know. To be honest, I'm not sure. It's complicated."

"Not trying to pry."

"Please, pry. It's no secret. It's . . ." She laughed. She looked at the man, standing uncomfortably, his eyes sad. "Can I sit?"

"Of course," he said, stepping to the wooden bench and sweeping some grit off with his hand. She sat and he pulled an old cane chair from the corner of the porch and sat too.

"That's why Matthew's been home alone," she said. Again, darkness in the eyes, but a big smile when they looked as if they'd turn black. "Ellie, she stays with my friends while I work, but Matthew's just too much of a handful for them."

The old man chuckled, thinking of the boy hurling rocks, climbing to the tops of trees, and jumping out of them.

"But he can take care of himself, and there's only a few more weeks till school starts."

"Sure."

"But it's comforting for me, knowing you're here."

The old man felt funny, annoyed that this family was depending on him, angry at the husband. Yet he felt a lightness too. They sat in silence. The old man cleared his throat. "Well, you tell the boy he can come here anytime. Just knock on the door like you did."

Her smile reminded him of June.

THE NEXT MORNING the old man lay awake in his clumpy bedding. He used to hustle out of bed at daybreak, his joints energized, hungry for work, his mind planning his day, June putting on coffee while he got dressed. But he had gotten in the habit of staying in bed till late in the morning, his mind blank, his body gumptionless, just lying, morbid and stone-like. He had slept poorly last night, excited about the mom and the boy, but also irritated.

He heard a soft knock. He put a robe on over his pajamas and opened the door. The boy stood there. "Hey, Matthew." The boy said nothing, just looked down at his feet. The old man started to regret his discussion with the boy's mother, but wasn't going to leave the kid standing there. "Okay. You can come in."

Matthew walked inside and began to roam around the house, stopping to tinker with a crescent wrench on a shelf, then wandering to the kitchen and picking up a jar of coins. "I'm going to make some breakfast. You want some?" said the man.

"Okay."

"Go around back to that chicken shed and go inside. In the nests are some eggs. You go get a few and bring them to me."

Matthew's eyes opened wide, and he ran out of the house. The old man put some butter in a pan on his stove, turned on the gas, and lit it. He took some bread out of the fridge and was going to put it in the toaster, but saw it was moldy, so he threw it out.

Matthew came back with a light-brown egg in each hand and gave them to the old man. "Good. Now go get a few more." Matthew went tearing out again.

On his return he ran up the front stairs and through the door, one of the eggs slipping out of his hand, flying through the air, and crashing to the floor. The old man sighed, thinking to himself this woman has a lot of nerve dumping her kid on me.

Matthew stood frozen, his hand over his mouth, his face turning red.

The old man looked at Matthew's round, shocked face, the egg splattered all over his living room, one slimy yellow splotch all the way to the kitchen. He started to chuckle, a house full of Goddamn egg because the boy's so excited. And the shocked looked on the boy's face got him laughing some more. And Matthew began giggling, too, at first tentatively, then merging with the old man's gruff merriment. And they stood there, just laughing, the sound echoing in the halls and vibrating in the walls of the lonely old house. ◇

White-Tailed Deer

Mary Johnson

What is common
Was once rare.

Was—
A silence at the edge
Of a meadow:
Two statues, ears pricked,
Scenting air,
The color of twilight.

Was—
Cloven prints, delicate,
In the mud by a stream, or
An oval nest, our size,
Pressed in the grass.

Was—
A flash of white, vanishing
Among the tree trunks,
Or, sometimes (not often),

A stately presence, tall-antlered,
Gazing at us.

This is what was:
Grandma pointing;
The deer (wild cattle) by the fence,
By the stream where the cows drank.
They were grace, silence, mystery.
They drew silence from me.
I had never, perhaps, seen deer before.

This is what they said to me:
Look.
Be still.
Listen.
Listen. ◇

Sundowning

Brendan Kiernan

I'VE GOT THIS WATCH THAT AUTOMATICALLY SYNCS ITSELF WITH A clock in Delaware every night at 2:00 a.m. A few times I've been up that late and seen it move by itself. It's got the hour and minute hands, too, it's not one of those digital ones with the lights blinking into different shapes. No, with my watch it's like something invisible is moving the hands. Our father had a watch that had Ferris wheel buckets in place of the numbers. With a magnifying glass we saw little animals—monkeys, puppies, giraffes—riding inside the buckets. Last night we fell back. I was up with indigestion and I saw the hands move one hour.

On the ramp leading up to the hospice doors there's a statue block-ing one of the porticoes. There she is—*mama, mama!*—mother of God staring down at me as I go past. Just before the magnetic strip that trig-gers the doors I stop. There I am in the brown glass: my belly has gotten bigger since I started my walks, my glasses are too big for my face, and last week I overheard a beautiful young woman on the train say that "almost no one looks good with a mustache." Something about the setup bothers me. I've been here before. I should just ignore this, touch the magnetic strip, go see Artie, and hope this feeling goes away. But the sidewalk also turns in either direction under perspectives of porti-coes. To my left, piles of leaves line the way to *Employee Parking*. To my right are more leaves bunched around little trees in big flowerpots. Sails on the water in the distance. The breeze is warm and spring-like even though the colors are all wrong. I step under the arch and into the bad painting.

It started in his esophagus although by the time it reached his liver—well, same old, same old. He wrote me a letter with the news. We live forty minutes apart and have multiple telephones. Yesterday I got another letter: he wants to see me. Other than that I had a hard time understanding what he was talking about. One sentence, he "accepts what's happening" and then the next, he's "adopted a bunch of seagulls" that gather at the same time every afternoon, and then there's "Carlina," his angel of a nurse, who sings and wipes him, and changed out of her uniform, right there in the room, when she thought he was asleep, but the pervert watched her through slit eyes while his "organs ached—I can't describe the pain, brother—I'm sundowning." Then he said he had been rereading Ayn Rand and that Carlina spoke Italian.

The hedges and mini-conifers hide me from the people on the back lawn. I'm on a curving path leading down to the water. The path is lower down than the lawn and twists in on itself as if it's figure-eighting me into the middle of something having to do with Artie. The ocean shelters the hospice grounds inside a bowl-shaped inlet at the bottom of the hill. I can't see the beach from here over the dunes and grass, just the narrow rock jetty covered in black birds. Behind me there are gaps in the little trees which let me see the people on the lawn. My head is at the level of their feet, making them seem like a cult of robed giants. I don't see my brother, maybe he was kicked out for violating its tenets. Some of them could be posing for devotional paintings, such as the bald woman pointing at the squirrel or the man removing his teeth on the lawn chair, and that's the best they could come up with for iconography. It's all very peaceful. There should be classical music playing as the sun shines down on them. A woman with Einstein's haircut keeps time to it as she leans into her nurse. What do they care what time it is? Time of their lives. No wonder why my brother's not out here: Artie the one-man party. Or maybe he's off with his Carlina.

I drove the forty minutes to see him after I got his diagnosis letter in the spring. On the phone Dot, my sister-in-law and Artie's third wife, had said to get there at noon, they should be back from Mass by then. We had sprung ahead the night before—I slept through my watch moving—and so I was an hour early. It takes me a while to adjust to change. In Venice the jet lag hit me three days after we got there and I slept in. My wife left a note saying to come and meet her, Dot, and Artie at a famous church at noon. It was already 1:00 when I woke up but I went there anyway and waited, walking under the porticoes and talking to the statues and pigeons until they came back for me. That wait was the best part of the trip. I thought about this in my brother's driveway looking up at his ridiculous cathedral window.

I'm almost to the point where the sidewalk turns to a dirt path. The walkways keep descending and so now I'm below the lawn against a stone wall. Someone above me is giggling. The sound slips over the wall and makes me stop. I climb back up a few paces. Standing on tiptoes and pulling myself up by the wall, I see a rough triangle of bare branches framing an old pair of feet and a young pair of hands. There's a smell of vanilla. The young hands have long fingers and freakish thumbs. One time my wife got me a pedicure. I hadn't realized it was also a lovely foot massage, although I haven't gotten around to another one yet. The freak fingers pull on twisted toes with black-crusted nails and then move to the soles and heels: every time the thumb slithers over the arch the giggling starts up again. More white lotion is spread over the top of the feet, disappearing into the skin like sweat beads in reverse and increasing the vanilla odor. I notice something move peripherally. There's a beetle perched on a branch watching with me: neighbors bumping into one another behind the curtain at the video store.

"Pancreas! Little friend! What are you two up to?" says a voice from somewhere behind the hands and feet.

"Hi, Liver," reply the feet.

"Technically, Esophagus—but my friends call me Esoph."

You've got to be kidding me. Time to go, I tell the bug.

INSIDE THE HOUSE I barely heard a word Artie said because I was distracted by his nose hair, his lone, friendless nose hair like a strand of squid-ink spaghetti reaching for his mouth. He's got one of those trimmers but he must have rushed it because of the news. Every time he paused for me to react I had to take my eyes off the hair and find the remnants of what he had just gotten off his chest. I did feel terrible for him, which was terrible for me as well because it was so unusual. Imagine hating seafood your whole life and then (true story) discovering linguine with clam sauce in your sixties. For part of the visit I was also seated on the long, cushioned bench that divides the entryway from the living room. I was facing the cathedral window with the big spring sky streaming in on a Sunday. Jesus, it felt like church on Easter just to be in his foyer, which is bigger than my living room. Dot rocked back and forth next to him when she was done bringing the sandwiches. He would say something like "I wish I had trusted the first opinion" or "Is that one of those watches that sync automatically?" and that hair would just dance back and forth under the output pressure from his nostrils, putting an extra second or two on every awkward moment of silence between us. Eventually we got on to the Giants and things settled down. The sun and clouds moved, changing the angle of light from heaven and finally removing the sky-blue spotlight from the hair. I felt bad that I hadn't said anything. All he would have had to do was go back into the bathroom for a minute and get out the trimmer. I normally would have but the shock of his situation made it feel like I'd be telling him something much worse. He did seem to relax, though, when we were talking about the Giants. His eyes uncreased and for a few minutes right before I left he looked like a younger version of our father. Dot pecked me on the cheek and Artie asked me if I wanted a water bottle for the ride home.

The paths all lead down to the beach. The one I'm on is lined with hedges broken up by bonsai trees planted in flowerpots. The smell of seaweed gets closer as you go down into the little ravines where the path turns. It's colder down here. The salt wind and sand sprays over the top of the tall grass. What are the chances? I mean, I know he's obviously at the hospice so he would be there somewhere, but what are the chances we end up a couple of yards away from each other while I'm trying to procrastinate? In his letter yesterday he mentioned that "sundowning" three times. It sounded like the place was a peaceful resort up to that point—the late afternoon, when everyone's energy starts to drain—and then the death and dementia turn it into a neighborhood you avoid after dark. The sun's going down, I should get back; maybe I'll even get to meet this Carlina. I've also timed this visit to avoid Dot, who said she would be here in the morning and back by sunset. And now I've spooked myself down here on the shingle. I'm afraid of sundowning myself. My shoes are off, the warm sand is between my toes, and my hands are in my strolling pockets, but I'm far from relaxed. That nagging voice, he is your brother, the sundowning, the black birds leaving one by one at the end of the jetty: all of this makes me check my watch even though there's no chance it moves by itself this time of day. Why? I find one of those metal pokers for spearing trash lying on the rocks. I'll use it as a walking stick weapon on my way back up the paths in case some invalid gets any ideas.

One time Artie left me stranded on an island. It was the summer we went to Canada, where it stayed light so long you couldn't tell what time it was. We left the campground one night for ice cream and came out of the shop into the middle of the morning. What happened with the island was that Artie borrowed a rowboat he found at the side of a river, and took me with him. We came to a creek that ran into the saltwater bay. We grounded the boat on a little marsh island and went swimming. I got stung by a jellyfish and my ankle swelled up so much it didn't fit into my soaked sneaker. I started to hyperventilate. He held me until I calmed down. I must have fallen asleep. When I woke up he wasn't there. The swelling had gone down but I was covered in bug bites. It was darker, I was convinced it was one in the morning and couldn't tell from the light. Artie's Swiss Army knife was sticking out of the sand next to me, covered in jellyfish slime. There was a trail of the flesh, like clear Jell-O mixed with rotted shrimp, running down to the indentation in the sand where the boat should have been. I stood by the water scratching myself in terror. Eventually I saw a motorboat with my father in the passenger seat. He let me wear his Ferris wheel watch on the ride back to the campground—I'd only been gone two hours—and gave me a bottle of calamine lotion. I remember imagining it was two in the morning and swirls of pink crust on my legs in a blue light.

Carlina looks like 1963 Claudia Cardinale's older sister if she ate a cheeseburger twice a week. Meaning perfect. She's got the dark wisps of hair over the forehead, dark eyes, and the sundown framing her silhouette. She's standing next to my brother with one hand on his wheelchair. Artie's staring at my metal spear as if he's sure I've just murdered someone with it. He looks like shit, a hollow, monkish shit that's been praying in a dark cave. There are two books in his lap, one fat and one skinny. He asks me if that was me running away from the hedges before. "I'll leave you two alone," Carlina says. I'm disappointed she doesn't have an Italian accent. "Just make sure you bring 'im back." If I wanted to hear the old neighborhood I could listen to my brother.

She indulges me, Leo, that's all there is to it. Stop looking at me like she's number four. Dot'll be back in an hour, she doesn't like her sneaking me out here. Really she's just jealous. What difference does indoors or outdoors make at this point? Let's walk.

That means you have to push, asshole.

Gentle, gentle . . .

Take a left down that little path. Shit. Back up. You see through that gap, see those rocks? That's where I keep my birds; I can see them through the window. They left early today. Must have slipped my mind with the time change. Messed me up real good an hour ago. How long have you been down here? Let me hold that. You a garbage collector now?

Did you ever notice how we talk the same when we're together, like we're kids again? I have. It sucks you back in. It's kind of . . . comforting. And embarrassing at the same time. I always wanted to escape. I know, I know, you know the feeling.

Right. No, I meant left, I meant the right—the correct—way, so go left. See that little sand outcrop like a wave with the grass on top? Carlina told me that's called witch grass but I think she made it up. Let's sit there out of the wind.

Oh, come on. I can get down myself. See that, that's a scarecrow. Me and Carlina made it out of driftwood. Arts and crafts in my old age, Leo. Now listen, have to tell you a story. A guy across the hall from me was called Pancreas. There's a new Pancreas now—there's only so many organs, the lowest on the totem pole are Colo-Recs, by the way. Anyway this first

Pancreas—his real name was Terry, I think—hardly said a word to anyone the whole time he was here. My bed was situated catty-cornered to his doorway so that I could see into his room. He was just this bag of skin propped up in bed writing postcards and sleeping and praying, once in a while he got cleaned up, morphine toward the end too, of course.

So, quiet guy, right? No visitors, none. Then one day right around now, sunset, four people show up. As far as I could make out it was brother, sister-in-law, nephew, and maybe cousin. Within five minutes they're screaming at each other about some shit that happened twenty years ago when Mommy and Daddy died and this one borrowed too much money and YOU SHOULD'VE CALLED ME and blah fucking blah. And him, he doesn't say a word. He's just raising his hand like, Excuse me, Garçon, Garçon! Check please! out into the hallway when Carlina walks by. She goes in and closes the door. I hear her voice, angry, I've never heard her angry before— what? Yes, yes, she sounds pretty damn good angry. Stop interrupting me, you fucking pervert. After a minute it's total silence. Then Carlina comes out with the four of them and leads them down to the cafeteria. The lamps are turned down by Pancreas's bed so I can barely make him out. I'm pretty sure his face is shaking and I'm thinking, oh, great, now he's going to start slobbering and they'll all come back. But he turns his head into the light and now I'm sitting up on my bed leaning over to get a better view of him—he's laughing, Leo, fucking laughing. Then he sees me see him and starts to laugh even more. You know how sometimes people catch laughing like a yawn? Well, this was not one of those times. That man creeped the hell out of me. It was like a zombie jack-o'lantern was making fun of me. He closed his eyes and died right then. Just needed the pains in the asses out of the way, I guess.

I have a book for you, I'd like you to read it.

This is sharp. You could spear a fish with this as well as a gum wrapper. Listen, I may not be in a position to ask you favors, but do me this favor. I want you to take this poker thing. Here, hold it tight, that's right. Now go kill me something.

I don't know. There's no jellyfish at this time of year. A little crab or something. Hurry up, it's getting dark.

Exit Artie.

My hands still smell like the ocean. On the way back he gave me the thin book (the fat one was Ayn Rand) and told me to read page 71. There was no beating of breasts or pulling of hair on the lawn when sundowning was supposed to happen. Maybe it all goes on inside. Carlina was waiting for us under a portico. She took him back inside like she knew what was going to happen.

I'm watching my watch. The numbers have been replaced by Ferris wheel buckets. My brother's jumping down from bucket to bucket going clockwise while the monkeys and giraffes and hippos go counter. He's wearing a porkpie hat and shouting something into a megaphone but I can't hear him.

"And to say that you're no longer here is only to say that you've entered another order," according to page 71.

My wife's holding my hand on the bed. It must be three in the morning. The phone rings. "Now what's so funny?" she asks me. ◇

Note: "And to say that you're no longer here . . . ": Eugenio Montale, "Visit to Fadin"

Ark

Holly Guran

Asleep in the ark of bed,
the wife, the husband, the dog
wrapped in bunched bedclothes
each with a special way
of breathing. Sometimes breath
signals from the dream—
a quickening of garbled words,
a sigh. Sometimes dreams
escape in the dark room.

Dead parents appear young,
able to talk and walk.
The dog whimpers remembering
her early confinement.
A friend returns with a message:
all you need lies within.

Bedded down, the pack rests
in warm touch.
The edges yield as the ark
rocks, retrieving the ones lost.
Beyond the room's windows,
a deep breath of stars
enters night's ocean. ◇

Tables of Four

Holly Guran

Peter piper picked a peck . . . mother's
    tongue is lightning with the twisters
she grins   wins again   our four palms overturning
slap and the cards are flying   they sit
    two couples *one club, pass, a spade—*
Jerry, time for a refill   the ashtray's stuffed
    three no trump!   she's exuberant

counting aces   the pad fills with numbers
    I don't see because they fade
like the couch where she drank rye and soda
    like the table where we four had dinner

one on each side   he's at the head
    serving meat with a long fork he raises after carving
she's at the other end dishing out the carrots, potatoes
    salad had its own plate off to the side

lucky salad   sister hides under the table
    until they scold her *come out* and scold her again
your dirty hands and I'm sitting
    there miss goody two shoes it makes me

want to puke   sister takes what they hand out   I'm
        no help   after the vanilla pudding's cleared   I go sit
on his lap   I still can't read mother's face saying
        you always were   daddy's girl ◇

Driver's Education

Madeline Hendricks

THE CHARACTERS

Dᴀɴ *(a 32-year-old cab driver)*

JoJo *(Dan's 8-year-old daughter)*

Wᴏᴍᴀɴ *(between 30 and 45 years old)*

Cᴀʟɪsᴛᴀ *(a 27-year-old runaway bride, decked out in full bridal wear from head to toe)*

Mᴀɢɢɪᴇ *(a 40-year-old businesswoman, Dan's former boss)*

The Woman, Calista, and Maggie could all be played by the same actor.

SCENE
Dan's yellow cab, in New York City

TIME
Early February 2009

There are four chairs center stage: two in front and two behind, making a car with two front seats and two backseats. At rise: DAN is driving the cab. JOJO is sitting in the front seat, bored. The WOMAN is a passenger in the backseat. JOJO tries to turn on the radio and DAN pushes her hand away.)

JoJo

Dad . . .

DAN
(Sternly)

JoJo.

(JOJO tries again, this time more secretly, but DAN catches her.)

JoJo

Dad!

DAN

JoJo.

JoJo
Oh, Dad, come on. I just want to listen to some music. I'm bored!

DAN
JoJo, give me a break. It's my first week on this damn . . . darn job. Is it too much to ask for a little peace and quiet?

JoJo
Fine. But you should have just left me home.

DAN
Well, I couldn't have. It's a snow day, and I wasn't going to leave you alone all day.

JoJo
Why? It would have been more interesting than this. *(She makes clucking noises with her tongue)*

WOMAN
You know what? You can just let me off here.

DAN

What? But your stop isn't for another ten blocks.

WOMAN

I know that. It's fine, I'll walk. Here you go. (*She hands DAN some money and exits.*)

DAN
(*Looking at the money*)
And no tip. Great. Look, Jo, I'm sorry you don't get to have fun on your snow day, but that doesn't mean you have the right to annoy my customers.

JoJo

I'm not annoying anyone! And we could have fun together if you would just turn on the radio.

DAN

I need peace and quiet, I told you.

JoJo

Okay.
(*Beat*)
You're so angry.

DAN

No I'm not.

JoJo

Yes you are.

DAN

No I'm not!

JoJo

Yes you are!

DAN

Well, that's what happens when the economy crashes and people lose their jobs. They get angry, all right?

JoJo

All right.

(Beat)

Can we go to the Central Park Zoo?

DAN

No, we don't have time.

JoJo

I've lived in New York my whole life and I've never been to the Central Park Zoo.

DAN

I'm working.

JoJo

I want to see the polar bears! They're my favorite, Dad, you know that.

DAN

We don't have time.

JoJo

But Dad . . .

DAN
(Yelling)

I said, no!

(visibly upset)

I'm sorry I yelled. I . . . Oh, look, a customer. . . Oh, my God.

(DAN pulls over.)

CALISTA
(Running and getting into cab)

Go!!!!

DAN

Excuse me?!

CALISTA

I said go! For God's sake, just drive! (DAN starts driving.) Could you

197

go any faster?

DAN

I'm sorry, ma'am, there's traffic.

CALISTA
(*On the verge of tears*)
Oh, God, oh, God, oh, God. What am I doing? I just left. I . . . I just left.

JOJO

Where did you come from?

CALISTA

He's never going to speak to me again. And my parents? And all the guests? There were three hundred people at that wedding, did you know that? Three hundred people-and I've never even met half of them! But I did like his parents, I did. They were the sweetest couple. Oh God, what am I doing?!

JOJO

Would you like to listen to some music? Maybe that will calm you down.

DAN

JoJo . . .

CALISTA

No. I can't deal with music right now.

JOJO

You sure? Music always helps me relax.

CALISTA

No, no, no . . . Maybe you're right. Music could be nice.

(*JOJO looks to DAN for approval and he nods. She turns on the radio. "Leaving on a Jet Plane" by Peter, Paul, and Mary comes on.*)

CALISTA

Oh, no, not this song. Anything but this song.

(JOJO switches to another station.
"Hallelujah" by Jeff Buckley comes on.)

CALISTA

Oh, God . . .

(DAN turns off the music and gives JOJO a stern look.)

DAN

I'm sorry, ma'am. This happens to be my very own take-your-daugh-
ter-to-work day.

CALISTA

Oh, it's fine, really. Completely fine. *(She bursts into tears)* Oh, Jesus,
I'm such a fucking idiot!

(DAN swerves on the road and then regains control. Car horns sound.)

JOJO

Dad, she said the "f" word.

DAN

I know, honey. Shhh . . .

CALISTA

It all just happened so fast! One day we're exchanging phone numbers
at a restaurant and the next he's down on one knee proposing. And
really, who could say no to a four-carat Harry Winston?

JOJO

Who's Harry Winston?

DAN

Shhh . . .

CALISTA

But he knew I wasn't ready! You know, he's the one who told me to move
in in the first place. And he's the one who developed a severe snoring
problem the minute we started sharing a bed. It's like, the instant I fell

199

asleep, he became a fucking human lawn mower. That could really drive a person crazy, don't you think? It's all his fucking fault!

(DAN swerves again. Car horns sound.)

DAN

All right, ma'am, please.

JoJo

Well, technically it's not his fault if he snores.

CALISTA

Okay, fine, but he still . . . I'm sorry, who are you?

JoJo

I'm JoJo.

DAN

Ma'am, do you have an address for me of some kind?

CALISTA

Oh, God, I'm such a mess. Just let me off at the next block.
(Beat)
I just single-handedly ruined my entire life, didn't I?

JoJo

Now don't say that.

CALISTA

He really loves me. He is actually in love with me and I . . .

JoJo

You . . . ?

CALISTA

I guess . . . I never really loved him. I got so swept up with the idea of being a bride that I forgot to double-check that I loved the groom.
(Beat)
But who said being in love was that important anyway? All a person really needs is someone to hold their hand when they're sad, I guess.

But I couldn't let myself have that. (*She searches for some money.*) Oh, God, I have no money on me. Ugh, shi . . . I mean Damn!

DAN

Don't worry about it. It's on me.

CALISTA

Oh, thank you. Thank you so much. (*As CALISTA exits, she screams to a person offstage.*) Oh, Mr. Pretzel man! I just ruined my entire life!

JOJO

Wow.

DAN

Wow is right. Poor girl.

JOJO

And you call me overdramatic.

DAN
(*Laughing*)

JoJo!

JOJO

What? She said she just ruined her life. That is so not true.

DAN

I guess you're right.

(*Beat*)

JOJO

Dad?

DAN

Yeah?

JOJO

Is that what happened with Mom?

DAN
(*Startled by the question and taking a moment to answer.*)

No, sweetie. Mom left long after the wedding day. And for different reasons.

JoJo

Why?

Dan

You know why, Jo, we've talked about this.

JoJo

Not really. You never really tell me. You always change the subject.

Dan

I do not.

(Beat)

So, how was that spelling test yesterday?

JoJo

You're doing it again.

Dan

Well, Jo, this is complicated.

JoJo

You always say that.

Dan

That's because it is! Look, Jo . . . Oh, wait, we've got another one.
(DAN pulls over. MAGGIE, gets into the cab.)

Maggie

Hi. Seventy-second and Lex, please—the big blue building.

Dan

Oh, my God.

Maggie

What? (Realizing who it is.) Oh, my God, Dan?

Dan

Maggie.

                    JoJo
I'm JoJo.

                    MAGGIE
Hi.

                    JoJo
Who are you?

                    MAGGIE
I'm . . .

                    DAN
She's my boss. Well, was my boss.

                    MAGGIE
Oh, Dan. I'm so sorry. You know we had no choice.

                    DAN
Hey, Maggie, it's fine.

                    MAGGIE
Okay. (*There is a long, awkward silence.*) So this is your daughter, I
presume?

                    DAN
That's her.

                    (*Silence*)

                    MAGGIE
And you're driving cabs now?

                    DAN
One of my many jobs right now. But yes. I'm a cab driver.

                    MAGGIE
That's great.

                    DAN
Yup.

JoJo

Want to hear some music?

Dan and Maggie

Yes.

Dan

What a great idea, JoJo! Why didn't you say that before?

(JoJo is elated and blasts the radio. "Money, Money" from Cabaret comes on. It is awkward. DAN shakes his head so JOJO will change it. "Money, Money, Money" by ABBA comes on.)

Dan

What station is this, Jo?

JoJo

I'm not sure.

Maggie

You know what—I'll just get out here. It's a freezing but beautiful day and I need the exercise.

Dan

Fine with me.

Maggie
(Giving DAN the money.)
Here you go. And here's some for you, GiGi. And you can both keep the change.

JoJo

Cool!

Dan

That's really not necessary.

Maggie

Please. It's the least I can do. Goodbye, Dan. And I really am sorry. We all are.

(*MAGGIE exits.*)

JoJo

That was awkward.

Dan

Just my luck. Of all the cabs in all the towns in all the world, she walks into mine. (*He looks up at the sky, as if talking to God.*) You having fun up there? I hope you're enjoying yourself.

JoJo

Who are you talking to?

Dan

No one. (*Beat*) Jesus. (*To God.*) How long is this going to go on for, huh?!

JoJo

Dad, what are you doing?

Dan

I'm just . . . looking for some answers, that's all.

JoJo

Looks like we both are.

Dan

What? Are you talking about your mom again? (*JOJO shrugs.*) You really want to hear this? Right now?

JoJo

I'm not that little anymore, Dad. I'm eight years old!

Dan

Oh well in that case . . .

JoJo

I'm serious.

Dan

All right. She was . . . sick. Not when I met her, but over the years.

And when she had you, she was so happy and grateful . . . and also scared.

JoJo

Scared? Scared of what?

DAN

Well, you were so perfect and innocent. I think she was scared she would ruin you.

JoJo

Cause she was sick?

DAN

Right. Sick in her brain. And she needed to go away in order to get better.

JoJo

Right.

DAN

But JoJo, listen to me. Your mother loved you so much. She loved you more than anything else in the world. It's because she loved you that she let herself go away and get help. It was all for you.

JoJo

If she loves me, then why doesn't she come back?

DAN

She's . . . the doctors said she's still sick. But she's trying very hard to get better.

JoJo

And maybe one day she'll come back?

DAN

Maybe. Maybe not. (*He takes JOJO'S hand and holds it tightly.*)

JoJo

That crazy bride lady was right.

DAN

What? Why?

JoJo

You holding my hand right now? It makes me feel better. We all just need someone to hold our hand, I guess.

DAN

You're very smart. All the money in the world couldn't teach you that.

JoJo

Everything's going to be okay, right Daddy?

DAN

Everything's going to be okay.
(*He looks at JOJO and then at the radio. He turns it on and a weather report comes on, spoken by an upbeat weatherman*)

WEATHERMAN
(*Voice-over*)

And a look at tomorrow's forecast: The snow storm continues. We can expect another six to eight inches by nightfall.

(*DAN and JOJO look at each other with panicked faces, and then smile. JOJO changes the radio station. "I Got You Babe" by Sonny and Cher comes on.*) ◇

Painting Flowers in Bellevue

John A. Black

The colors are pure:
Like salt or rain.
Lucent summers wax and vanish.
A virulent winter roars out
Of silence and dissolves into azure.

This is the woman who walked on the moon.
She talks of seizures and of lights
That flicker in the corridors.

I explain, for my part, that I arrive
With only a chaplain's solace;
I hold a trembling hand and I tremble.

She tells me about her pilgrimage.
Then she paints and flowers bloom.
Sunflowers gold and Nubian.
Lilacs with a tint of Mars.
She squints toward the window
Too thick with earthly dust

For her to see the river beyond.

Lying back, she hands me a rock
As porous as coral and bellows:
"Keep the faith . . . "

She reminds me of snow in early April:
Radiant white and startling.
She reminds me of a child
Who wanted the moon once, long ago, too.

And her flowers, like her words, endure. ◇

A Good Enough Dog

Julie Broad

"**W**E COULD FAIL," DAVE TOLD ME. "WE AREN'T MAKING money. The bed-and-breakfast never worked. We're getting tired." He leaned forward, putting his elbows on his knees, getting closer to the wood-burning stove. The firelight etched the creases deeper into his forehead.

"But here," he continued, "I'm happy. I eat food I grow. I live in my own house. The only thing I need to buy is beer." He took a sip. Rock Bottom Brewery.

Dave owns the farm and B&B with his partner, Connie. I get room and board in exchange for working and helping with guests, though they are few. The couple lived in Baltimore until they grew tired of it and decided to move to the Maryland countryside. Dave is a climatologist, Connie a thespian. Julie and Janine, a middle-aged lesbian couple and our only regular guests, often sit in the living room and look over our shelves for titles such as *Minerals of Western Pennsylvania* and *Theater and Sexuality*. Dave teaches me how to shoot guns and drive the Kawasaki—a glorified golf cart we use for transporting wood and tools around the farm. He seems determined to teach every girl who works on the farm as much about manhood as possible. Connie likes teaching me everything, especially things I already know.

Kaya, the dog, walks through the living room to sit at Connie's feet. Connie is standing in the doorway of the living room. She is a lofty character, despite her modest stature. She gets on her knees, and scratching Kaya behind the ears, finds a tick. Kaya usually plays in the woods behind our house and always brings home ticks.

"Oh, my. You are a good dog. You are a very good dog. You are a good enough dog." When Connie says this, she means it. The tick is removed, and Connie leads Kaya into the kitchen for dinner.

I look back at Dave, who is still hunched over. His eyes are a watery gray, which adds to the illusion that he is both a heartbroken boy and a man of emotional might, his words carrying his heart. He does shooting practice in the back garden and comes inside for lemon tarts or tiny chocolate-chip cookies. He'll pop one into his mouth, leave the room, and when he thinks no one is looking, turn around and get another with a mischievous smile. He collects firearms from World War II and builds cardboard houses for his cat, Badger.

But he is a serious man. He needs to be physically able to control the animals, as well as heavy machinery. He makes a hobby of guns, and despite this, doesn't have any medical insurance. In the late fall, Dave and I were moving the beehives onto a more level platform, getting the bees ready for winter. Dave was wearing a full beekeeper's outfit, and I was wearing a mesh mask, standing farther away. He was dismantling the hive. Each removed section exposed more bees to the cold. They didn't like their house being taken down, and found their way into his suit. He yelled for me to leave. I looked back, got stung, and saw him rushing into the tall grass, shedding his suit. I didn't know which was worse, being exposed to all the bees in theory, or being exposed to a few bees that are locked inside your clothes in actuality.

I waited for him in the house. When he came in, he had three welts on his face, and wasn't wearing pants. He sat down and let his head fall back against the wall. "I'm allergic to bees," he said, looking at the ceiling.

One of his eyes was shut for the next two days, his fingers had swollen like sausages, and when he opened his good eye, he couldn't see straight. Connie and I worked double time, picking up his chores.

When we would come inside, he would stare at us blindly.

Surely, his life couldn't be that happy.

One morning, Dave went to feed the pigs, but they were gone. I woke up to the crunch of gravel as the Kawasaki zoomed past my room in the barn. I caught a glimpse of Dave, enough to see that he was still wearing his bathrobe, and had only pulled on his faded white sneakers and his florescent orange hunting cap. He was hunched over the steering wheel. Connie knocked on my window, where I already had my nose to the glass. "The pigs are gone," she trilled. She started walking away, and over her shoulder said, "But you can stay in bed if you really want to." She was halfway down the driveway by the time I pulled my shoes on. I said nothing when I caught up with her, and we just walked. Kaya loved the early morning jaunt, and when we passed the pigpens—where the fence was indeed down—she trotted into that previously closed section of the woods. She found a wallowing hole, full of pig shit and food and mud and old apple cores that had been throw in for the pigs. She dived in. I laughed, thinking of the mess she would be. I didn't think Connie would approve. She doesn't clean other people's messes. Kaya ran back, all tongue and tail. She sat at Connie's feet, and whined in pleasure as Connie said, "Yes, you're a good dog. You're a very good dog. You're a good enough dog."

We continued walking. Pigs are foraging animals, and they go every which way in search of grubs. We saw broken branches and deep trenches where the pigs' noses cut through the dirt, and we followed. Connie knew the pigs would come back. "The pigs need us. They won't go far. They're social animals and they'll want to come back." I couldn't disagree. The pigs loved belly rubs (what we called bacon-rubs), especially Rose and Lily, our pregnant sisters. The independence might be less comfortable.

Dave found the pigs. The sound of the Kawasaki means getting fed and watered, and bacon-rubs, and they no doubt ran to him as soon as they heard him coming. "They're in the next property over. Go back and get the apples and corn and we'll bring them back." We spent the rest of the morning luring the pigs home with treats. A couple of hours were spent repairing the electric fence, its wires frayed where the pigs had burst through. Once we were in the kitchen and had each had enough coffee, Dave chuckled. "Well, that's one way to wake up."

The week after, we delivered Amy—our beloved, seven hundred-pound pig—to the meat locker. Amy had been at the farm for as long as Dave and Connie had owned it. Dave said a prayer. "We have sustained you, and now you shall sustain us. May your soul go freely to what comes next." He said that to every animal he brought to the slaughterhouse, whether it was a good friend or a pain in the ass. And he said it to them face-to-face. Amy wasn't supposed to go, though. We were trying to load Lance—her brother—into the trailer; he was the one with the appointment. But he wouldn't go. No matter how many apples and corncobs we gave him, he knew something was amiss. But Amy was a sucker for treats, and she barreled right in. Dave looked at me. I looked at Amy. She was Dave's baby, his sweetheart on the farm. "Shut the gate."

Amy came back in pieces from the slaughterhouse two days later, weighing in at 502 lbs. Neighbors came over to help with processing. We made sausage, bacon, and ribs, and we rendered the lard. She was treated well, Amy, and her meat showed it. The morning after, we had lard biscuits and breakfast sausage. "Amy," Dave said. "You taste damn good."

Dave's life is rich with losses. Some are staggering, some are just frustrating or tiring. He can walk into the garden to find that every bush bean has been eaten and curse the motherfuckers responsible, and there's nothing to do except start over. That's why the coffee is strong and the dogs are good. Rather, good enough. ◇

Tin Cup, Tin Plate

Gillian Lynn Katz

A white girl with white hands
places a tin cup of milk tea
and four sugars
on the back doorstep
of her family's house.
And a tin plate with sliced bread
(each piece thick as a brick)
smothered in raspberry jam.

The garden boy, Phineas,
eats behind the house
sitting on the ground.
White sheets flap
above him
on the washline.

The white girl stays locked in
behind barred windows.
Alarm wires thinly strung
across transparent panes.

Broken glass
cemented into high stone walls
surround, protect,
her childhood home.

And Phineas sits
in the backyard.
The white sheets flap
above him
on the washline. ◇

eGoli

Zulu name for City of Gold, Johannesburg

Gillian Lynn Katz

The leaping arc of linked impala
a sculpture curved
over a rainbow fountain
has been stolen
piece by piece.

Hacksawed, sold as scrap metal
in the New South Africa.

Oppenheimer Park in Johannesburg
built between President and Pritchard
before the bloodless revolution

stands empty. ◇

You're the Doctor

Douglas Krohn

THERE WAS A TIME IN NEW YORK WHEN MEN WORE FEDORAS TO WORK and neckties to the theater. There were shoe repair shops on every block, doctors smoked in public, and uptown there lived an internist named Blinderman, who dodged checkered cabs on his way to making house calls. He was a young man starting out, and his father—who had sold sock garters off an Essex Street sidewalk—convinced him it wasn't so bad getting paid in cash and tomatoes. Blinderman knew he could've been looking for a Park Avenue practice or starting one of his own. But his parents seemed content just to have a doctor for a son, and, thinking he'd be satisfied with their contentment, he denied himself the ambition to look for something grander. So he took an ad out in the *Herald Tribune*, sat in his one-room apartment, and waited for the phone to ring.

Usually he stared at his roommate, a refrigerator, whose white enamel door bubbled from a ceiling leak the super never fixed. Loneliness made him hungry, but when he opened his companion he found mostly condiments. The place needed a woman's touch: the mustard jar wouldn't open because the seeds had gotten thick around the cap. There was a tin of sardines on the shelf, the fish lying inside like in an open casket. A single olive lay at the bottom of its jar, having cried the pimiento out the top of its head.

217

Blinderman walked down York Avenue thinking about the patient he'd just seen. Ida Gelbman. Her room was thick with heat, and he'd found her leaning out a window, sucking in the air as if she were hungry for it. He fumbled for a stethoscope in his black leather bag. Ida's chest was like cellophane, her heart hissing like a steam press. He gave her water pills and when they started working she urinated so loud Blinderman heard it through the bathroom door. Ida came out of the bathroom smiling, but he knew she'd call again tomorrow.

He plodded home to wait for more calls. The air got hotter as he walked up to his room. He was opening his door when the housewife across the hall came out of her apartment and smiled at Blinderman. She was pretty in her yellow sundress, the perspiration of the late afternoon shining on her cleavage. He smiled back and watched her walk away. In between her heel clacks he was tempted to seize her from behind, but she vanished down the stairwell before he could act.

When he opened his door his face felt as if he were checking a roast. He opened his windows and surveyed his room. The bed was unmade, his radio's volume knob broken, the only sound was a bus pulling its achy frame from a street corner. If you'd spoken to him he would've said the whole world was alone in a hot room, stifled and barely breathing.

And then the phone rang.

"Thank goodness you're in, doctor! You've no idea what I been through."

The gravel voice sounded like one of his father's uncles, but they'd all passed away: Victor, Benny, the others. The voice stirred a memory of the family sitting shivah when he was a boy—first for Uncle Frank, years later Uncle Arthur. His father yelled at him for sitting on a box they put on the floor, so he weaved his way through the old people's legs until he was alone in a dining room.

His chin didn't come up much higher than the buffet. There was a whitefish lying on a platter, its skin brown and withered, its dead eye staring at him. He pulled the eye from its head and tried to chew it. He gagged immediately, spitting it back on the platter by the fish's tail. The eye stared at him again, dimpled by his baby teeth.

"Can I help you?" Blinderman said into the phone.

"God bless you, you've already helped. It helps to know you're listening."

In the background Blinderman heard a commotion.

"Are you calling from a public phone?"

"An emergency room. And let me tell you, doctor, they need more help than me!"

"I'm a physician who makes house calls, sir," said Blinderman.

"My father they call 'sir.' Me they call Manny. Last name Shapiro."

Blinderman couldn't shake the feeling he was on the phone with his past, though he knew no Shapiros.

"I'm sorry, but I don't have hospital privileges."

"So who says you'll see me in a hospital? I been stuck in this one three hours and *the doctors here* don't see me. So maybe you meet me at home?"

Blinderman looked at a photograph on the folding table where he had his meals: a picture of his father watching him build a snowman. His father's brow rose like a parabola, head tilted back, braced as if to prevent his eyebrows from losing their wonder should the little boy fall from promise and join him amongst the ordinary.

"Mr. Shapiro, you haven't told me what's wrong."

"What's wrong is I could plotz in this waiting room right now and no one would notice. They'd stick me in a corner and put me out with the trash. No one would know the difference—except now maybe you. So? You'll make me a house visit, or you going to allow God-knows-what?"

He hardly heard Shapiro; he was distracted by the picture, his father bent on one knee and looking much like Blinderman did now. The snowman stood between them. A row of radishes, curved like a belly-down C, was stuck in the snowman's head, and so it grinned, wait-ing for the carrot nose that the boy held in his hand.

"I suppose I could fit you in," said Blinderman, speaking to the picture. "Tell me where to go."

When Shapiro answered, Blinderman recorded the address, though he neglected to state his fee.

THE DOOR to Shapiro's apartment opened so soon after Blinderman pressed the buzzer that Shapiro must have been peering through the keyhole, waiting like an expectant child. At first glance, Shapiro reminded Blinderman of a gnome: his figure was compact, his bottom lip pouted, his eyebrows arched high, as if relaxing them might make him lose sight of the bogeyman he tracked from the corner of his eye. But he smiled when Blinderman sat down on the sofa, and if not for all that gray, you might've thought him a kid grown too big for his age.

"Would you like a glass of tea?" asked Shapiro.

"Isn't it a little hot for tea?"

"You prefer a glass of water maybe?"

Blinderman was accustomed to more panic—like when the Berkowitz girl was doubled over her belly. But this was like a social call: Shapiro's shirt was ironed crisp, violets sat on the window sill, and from a radio Red Barber lilted through the evening heat.

"I'm fine, Mr. Shapiro. How can I help you?"

"Good question. How about you give me my breath back?"

A pool of spittle shone on Shapiro's bottom lip, and Blinderman hoped he'd tuck it back into his mouth. But the lip sort of hung there, and again Blinderman thought of his great-uncles, old men with European customs, greeting him with a kiss on both cheeks. They'd sit in the living room speaking Yiddish, filling his ears with wet whispers of the success he'd be, the money he'd make, the pride he'd bring them, and Blinderman, disgusted by their age and cold pragmatism, would wipe away their saliva and dry his hands on his slacks.

"You've lost your breath?" asked Blinderman. "You have enough to fix me tea."

"So I'm polite—*that means I'm well?*" asked Shapiro, throwing his arms out wide to demonstrate his decay. "*And when I'm sick I'll be rude to doctors?*"

"I'm just saying you look good."

"So I look good. *One* person thinks so. But I feel like something's in my chest. A *beating.*"

"You *do* have something in your chest," said Blinderman, smiling as kindly as he could. "It's your *heart*, Mr. Shapiro."

"If it's my heart, doctor, then why am I so aware now? All my life I've had this heart and never did I feel a single beat."

Blinderman loosened his tie. "It's probably the heat. You should open some windows."

"If that's what you say—*you're the doctor*. But don't you want to take a look? Just take a look, doctor. Could it hurt to be safe?"

A large deco mirror hung on the wall across the room. Three black lines ran around its border. Along the left border a pink flamingo stood on one skinny leg. The glass was spotted with white dust, and Blinderman saw himself peeking through a cloud. He thought about Hippocrates and Maimonides, and his parents *kvelling* when he graduated school, but he couldn't deny Shapiro's intuition: he didn't want to touch him.

This shook him some. *Could it be that he had no more compassion than his uncles?* Through the mirror's reflection he awoke to a feeling that, deep inside, the only desire he consistently maintained was to honor his parents—two people remarkable only in their sturdy devotion to each other, and who represented to the other (just as Blinderman viewed medicine) nothing more than a practical choice.

He thought of this as he listened to Shapiro's heart, the older man sitting beside him on the sofa. It bothered him that Shapiro had his shirt on—he'd been taught to put his hands on the patient directly— but the last thing he wanted was Shapiro to disrobe. Everything bothered him a little—his craft, his patients, his own dusty image in the mirror—and the more he ruminated the more the sounds in Shapiro's chest pattered away from him, rising toward the ceiling, and soon the heart he was listening to was his own.

"How's it sound?" Shapiro blurted. "Am I going to make it?"

Blinderman put down his stethoscope. "I can't find anything wrong. You seem to be in perfect health."

Shapiro rose, his lips stiff and fortified.

"Then this is cause for celebration!" He started for the kitchen. "I made a chicken soup. I'll heat you up a bowl right now."

Blinderman cleared his throat. "I already ate."

"Don't worry, I put in *kreplach*, you'll find your appetite."

"I'm sorry, I have to get going."

Shapiro heard the 'no' in Blinderman's apology. "I understand, doctor. You a busy man, running around half the city caring for some *meshuggener*."

Blinderman looked in the mirror. "You know, Mr. Shapiro, there's something I need to discuss."

Shapiro beamed. "What's that, *boychik?*"

Blinderman fell silent. It had been years since he heard that. He thought of his grandfather holding his hand in Prospect Park. *Boychik*. From a stranger it felt like a dirty hand wiping itself on his sleeve. He stood up and snapped his bag shut.

"I'm sorry," said Shapiro. "I mean '*doctor*.' Forgive me, you're such a nice young man—it's like you're familiar."

Blinderman straightened his tie. "My fee is fifteen dollars."

"Fifteen dollars? Now I know why you study so hard. But I don't have that money."

Blinderman looked at the crystal vase on the coffee table.

"A gift from my mother," Shapiro said. "An heirloom."

"Then what do you have?"

"Right now, nothing. But send me a bill and I pay you back." Shapiro put up a finger as if to say "stay put" and disappeared into his kitchen. He re-emerged holding a box of beer pretzels. "In the meantime, doctor, you take this as payment. You go home and enjoy them—*with your family*."

Blinderman had no chance to refuse. The pretzels had made their way into his arms before he realized it. Somberly, he inspected the box, crushed on its top, flattened on its corners. Shapiro smiled proudly. Blinderman didn't know what to do except bid Shapiro's awkward hospitality farewell. He returned home to his refrigerator. The air in the stairwell was still thick. He loitered in the hall, waiting fruitlessly to catch the housewife across the hall in passing. Sitting at his table, he threw out his shoulder opening the mustard jar, but finally got it unscrewed and spread it on the pretzels, which he ate for dinner.

THE SUMMER HEAT SUBSIDED, but when the leaves turned, the telephone almost never rang. Once Blinderman was called to retrieve a pebble from a girl's nose, but his forceps didn't have teeth and he couldn't grasp it and in the end he sent the child to the emergency room. Sometimes, on a walk along Third Avenue, he'd run into an old classmate. One was on staff at Doctors Hospital, another in practice on West End, and when they handed him a business card Blinderman couldn't tell if they were offering consultation or counsel.

On one walk he found an old punching bag on the curb waiting for the garbage men. It had taken great effort to cradle the bag's awkward mass up the stairs, and still more to mount it on the ceiling—such investment for an object that only moved when pushed by others. In its pendulous travels, Blinderman thought, the bag had acquired nothing more than the odor of someone else's rank labor.

One sleepless night he began to hit the heavy bag. It moved a few inches on its suspension, but returned stubbornly to his chest. In the darkness he perceived the bag as his own silhouette, silent and inert, hung by himself in effigy. Smelling his sweat in the leather, he wondered how something so heavy could be swayed by the shove of a skinny man, the direction of a mother's hand, the stream of an old man's whisper. Blinderman closed his fists and punched. He took three-inch hooks, like those he learned in the Army, then abandoned technique and started swinging wild: crosses, uppercuts, combinations—all as if he were swinging to open a rent in the bag and let out more than sand.

When the phone rang at half past four, Blinderman had collapsed into a dream. He first put the speaker to his ear, then turned the receiver and mumbled into the phone.

"Doctor, did I wake you? It's me, Manny."

"I don't know any Mannys."

"Sure you do. Manny Shapiro. I had a beating in my chest."

"Yes," sighed Blinderman. He held his watch to the window and read it in the streetlight. "Is there a problem?"

Shapiro exhaled dramatically. "When isn't there a problem? The beating is back, but now worse. Like a palpitation."

"Then you should go directly to a hospital."

"And do what? Die like a dog in a waiting room?"

"If it's that serious, Mr. Shapiro . . . "

"What's the matter?" Shapiro interrupted. "You don't do house calls no more?"

"It's four-thirty in the morning. Can't this wait?"

"How should I know? You're the doctor."

You're the doctor. It always sounded like a case of mistaken identity: strange voices, usually kind, calling under the false presumption that Blinderman was a doctor. At least that's what it felt like. He'd had his own helpless memories of being a patient—his parents bringing him to the doorstep of an old man's brownstone in the middle of the night, his chest croupy, the doctor gathering him up like a bag of laundry and sitting with him in the steam of his shower room until the barking passed. Or the surgeon who saved his testicle, his father telling him the day before it was a muscle pull, just lie still and rub it. A lot of good it did him now, but the surgeon was kind, and the old doc before him, and he felt a sense of debt. Yet when he snapped shut his leather bag every morning he couldn't stop wondering if the license inside was a forgery. *You're the doctor.* It sounded like a plea for mercy, a midnight wail, resonant and rhythmic—*you're the doctor, you're the doctor, you're the doctor* . . .

"I'll be right over. Just give me some time."

"Bless you, doctor!" said Shapiro.

The stairwell was cold, the early autumn morning made Blinderman shiver, and as he descended he couldn't tell if it was his joints creaking or just the stairs. Outside he knew it wasn't summer anymore: he could no longer smell garbage rising off the sidewalk. He walked down Lexington. Tiny feet scratched against the metal pails and shadows moved along red-brick alleys, but by the time he got to Shapiro's building the streets were clean and the storefronts swept. The doorman let him in, and this time Shapiro was waiting in his doorway. His pajamas were neat—they had gold stripes—and his robe crisp. He wore slippers.

"Thank God you made it, doctor. Only a *mensch* comes at this hour."

"How are you feeling?" Blinderman walked directly to the sofa.

"A little better. But still . . . " He opened his palms upward. "Just to be safe."

"*Just to be safe?*" Blinderman rubbed away a pebble of sand from his eye. "What do you mean, just to be safe?"

The color drained from Shapiro's face.

"Why so angry, doctor?"

"Because I'm not a cop. I don't walk the streets at night so you can feel safe."

"It's my fault the palpitations go away? You should be happy."

"I was happy in bed."

Shapiro hunched his shoulders.

"You're not also happy with healing?"

"Healing what, Shapiro? Healing who?"

Shapiro gave Blinderman that familiar pout.

"Me for one, doctor. And your other patients beside."

"Just give me your hand."

He took Shapiro's wrist and pressed his pulse. He saw perspiration bead on the border of Shapiro's lips, and some on his brow, and he looked awfully pale, so who could know? He listened with his stethoscope. The beat was muted by ribs and sternum, but the rhythm was steady between the soft exchanges of air. Blinderman removed his stethoscope.

"What did you have before bed?"

"A glass of tea maybe."

"So don't have tea before bed. The caffeine makes your heart race and keeps you up."

"That's *exactly* my problem," said Shapiro, springing to his feet. "My heart races all night and I'm awake when I should be sleeping. Who knew a glass of tea? Coffee, certainly, but tea?"

"Now you know."

"And I feel better knowing. How can I repay you?"

Blinderman saw himself in the flamingo mirror. "How about my fee?"

"You want to stay for breakfast maybe?"

"No, thank you. Just my fee."

Shapiro plopped back down onto his couch. He exhaled, as he did before delivering any self-concocted drama, and Blinderman considered it all a performance: the pallor, the palpitations, the perspiration, the whole dog-and-pony show like Second Avenue theater.

"Then we got a problem, doctor. I don't have cash, and no checks neither."

"Enough's enough, Shapiro. You didn't pay me last time."

"You tell me, doctor, where do I get money at this hour?"

"Maybe stashed beneath the bed."

"All's there is cobwebs. I can't afford a dust ruffle."

"Safety comes at a price, Shapiro. You want to *just be safe* at this hour, think about it before you pull me out of bed."

"You're mad, doctor, I understand. But I make it up to you." Shapiro disappeared into his bedroom. After several moments of drawers opening and closing, he returned with a stack of magazines in a paper bag. "Send me a bill for both visits and I pay you back. Meantime, accept this as a gift."

First stale pretzels, now old magazines, but the whiff of both—an odor of dusty cardboard—triggered the same unease. Here he was again, *shtupped* by Shapiro, his urgent neediness, his cheapskate ways. Walking home he felt like a city tourist, pockets empty after falling for a three-card monte.

The sun peered above the river. Blinderman's eyes were swollen, watery. He blinked when he arrived home, his vision cleared—and there she was: the woman from across the hall, standing in front of their building. She wore an overcoat and guarded an assembly of packed boxes. Her face appeared fuller than before. In this pleasant imperfection Blinderman sensed a vulnerability, an approachable quality he couldn't dare detect when her cheekbones were barely veiled and her chin cast a modest shadow on her neck. He found the courage to speak.

"So I see you're moving."

She squinted at him, though the sun was at her back. She looked over her shoulder, her jaw jutting with tension, and before it got too uncomfortable Blinderman offered an introduction.

"Oh, yes," she said, relieved, and tipped her head in acknowledgment of the boxes on the sidewalk. "We're moving."

"Your husband—his job takes you someplace new?"

"No," she laughed. "We're staying local. We just need another room."

Blinderman rubbed his morning beard. "Someone moving in with you?"

"I suppose so—*kineahorah*." She laughed again, and in catching her breath her overcoat opened a crack. She looked down between the buttons of her coat, and with her palms cupped the small lump in her belly.

His ears were suddenly deaf to the sputtering diesels of garbage trucks and buses, his neighborhood block jaundiced and spinning. When the woman's husband pulled to the curb in a moving van, Blinderman clutched the stack of magazines and trudged upstairs.

He couldn't sleep. The sun burned through the blinds. Columns of darkness slanted across the room, their order as precise as prison bars. Blinderman tried to position his eyes within their widths, but each fitful turn on the pillow and his eyes moved back to a parallel of light. On the street below, the day started anew: a newsstand owner threw piles of tabloids on the sidewalk, each thud climbing to his window; men with wet cigars let out exaggerated laughs.

Lying in bed he reached for the magazines. He had seen this stuff in the Army. A girl folded out of the middle of each issue. The pictures brought him no closer to slumber, but eventually he was distracted by an article on Adlai Stevenson, and his eyes closed before he finished reading.

THEN IT WAS WINTER.

There hadn't been a call in days, not since a drunk hit his head at a Christmas party. The wind whistled off his window and he looked outside at an early Sunday morning. He hadn't thought about it before, but suddenly it struck him funny that someone had bothered to plant a tree across the street. The trunk sat in a square of hard dirt, carved out of the space between the curb and a sidewalk slab. The skinny branches were naked and didn't sway, as if the winds had abandoned them. He opened the window and stuck out his head, surprised to see that the block was lined with trees just like it. The city, apparently, was full of them.

The telephone rang. Blinderman closed the window.

"Hello?"

"Doctor—I've given up tea."

The voice was nearly breathless, gathering itself like a moth-eaten bellows, its wheeze slow and thready.

"Shapiro, is that you?"

"I feel like a boy cried wolf. I don't blame you for not believing."

"*I believe*," Blinderman pleaded. "Tell me what's the matter!" In an instant Blinderman was consumed by thoughts: that he hadn't seen what he'd been looking at all along, that he'd missed a clubbed finger on Shapiro's hand, or a pallid tinge in his eye, and in his omission he'd perpetrated something horrible. His throat was dry, so narrow that air could barely pass. He waited for a response, but the receiver was silent. "Is it your chest, Shapiro? Tell me, Manny! The palpitations again?"

"Yes." The bellows slowly expanded. "But this time tight. The sides of my eyes I see black."

"What do you mean black?"

"I ain't good. I maybe passed out."

"Then stay put," Blinderman ordered. "I'm coming over."

The streets were empty, the colorless sky his alone to breathe. Its bitterness stung his chest. It reminded him of the Army—basic training on a frozen field—and for the first time he smiled at the memory. All he had to do then was follow orders, and suddenly that seemed like such an easy place to be. He arrived at Shapiro's building nearly breathless, bounding past the doorman, past the elevator, and up the stairs to the eighth floor.

The door to Shapiro's apartment was ajar. Blinderman heard a faint gurgling behind it. He threw it open and rushed in, but was stopped cold by the scene before him. Shapiro was clean-shaven in a cardigan, standing behind a buffet. It was dressed with cloth and covered by a Sunday morning bounty: a basket filled with bagels, tubs of cream cheese, some peppered bluefish, sliced Nova. Blinderman smelled coffee drifting in from the kitchen—the gurgling was a percolator.

"Shapiro, what's all this?"

"I made us a brunch."

"You just called me on the brink of death. You told me you weren't doing good."

"I wasn't. What can I tell you? I hear your voice, I feel better. You should be proud."

"I'm not proud. I'm a *fool*."

"Why so hard on yourself, doctor? Sit down and eat. You'll feel better."

Shapiro pulled out a chair, and his fork was halfway into the bluefish, but before he could sit Blinderman's hand came down like a gavel on the table.

"I suppose that's today's payment, Shapiro—a plate of lox?"

"There's whitefish, too . . ."

"Enough, Shapiro! You don't need a doctor. You never did."

"All due respect, a man knows when he's ill."

"You were fine!"

"*After* I saw you, doctor, not before."

"I'm a fool. Like a child three times I fell for your perversions."

Shapiro pointed a sterling serving fork at Blinderman.

"You watch what you say!"

"You have some nerve, Shapiro, telling me to watch what *I* say. This is the end of the line." He held out his hand. "My fee, please, and then I'm on my way."

"But I don't . . ."

"Don't tell me you have no money—not with your doorman building and marble lobby. Don't slip off into that back room to pay me with . . . who knows, a bowl of subway tokens."

"Fine," said Shapiro. The serving fork kept Blinderman at a distance. Shapiro's other hand reached into his front pants pocket. He pulled out a silver clip, monogrammed and polished, the metal fatigued by a thick wad of twenties. Shapiro pulled out three, crumpled them, and threw them at Blinderman's feet. "Here you go, doctor, one for each visit—*with interest*. And now you're a whore like the rest!"

Blinderman stood still, pale and apprehensive. As Shapiro glared, he wondered why the older man's words stung so much. It was Shapiro who was the crazy one—he *knew* this, like he knew his own name. Yet an impulse ripped through him, a sensation that unsettled his gut and surged like a current in the part of the brain that is more convenient to never know, and it told him he deserved the scorn. Blinderman trembled. He tried to steady himself by picking up the crumpled bills, but he continued shaking.

"It's always the same," Shapiro cried over him. "A prescription and a bill, or else nothing! Would it have hurt, doctor, to offer *meaning*? One lousy time you couldn't lend a fella *dignity*?"

Blinderman hurried out of the apartment, Shapiro's words on his trail. He escaped into the elevator and the doors closed. He looked at the panel above the door. The floor numbers lit up as he descended, but the fourth-floor bulb was blown, and while he stared at the unlit number he heard Shapiro's voice resonate. *Meaning* and *dignity*. Millions of people, he thought, and Shapiro should seek these virtues in a house call.

Blinderman looked down at his leather bag. It had come unclasped. The bell of his stethoscope stuck out, and he thought of the day his parents had given it to him. He remembered his difficulty suppressing a smile the first time he slipped it in his ears and pressed it against a stranger's skin. And in that moment of pride, remembered he realized what it was that he had been seeking in medicine: *meaning* and *dignity*. He looked up at the round mirror in a corner of the elevator car. His face was magnified, narrow, his body tiny and distorted, but he was undeniably looking at himself.

The elevator door opened and he staggered toward the lobby doors. Outside on the sidewalk he saw a man and his son. The child was on a bicycle with training wheels, probably a Christmas gift, and the father guided him through the bitter cold day. The boy laughed when the wind blew him off his bike, and his father tenderly brushed off his knees.

Blinderman watched them pass, then turned around and made the long climb back to the eighth floor. ◇

CONTRIBUTORS

Raymond Philip Asaph is a Long Island furniture mover, so if you've moved to Westchester from Nassau or Suffolk, it's possible he moved you. He was educated at Eckerd College, Bucknell, and NYU, and on trucks all over the tri-state area. Tell him how his story made you feel at *longislandwriter@gmail*.

Carlyn Attman is a recent graduate of Vassar College with a degree in English. She is currently navigating the misty post-collegiate world with a fantasy novel in one hand and a mug of tea in the other. Any and all ideas for future pursuits may be sent to *carlyn .attman@gmail.com*

Peggy Aylsworth lived in Yonkers during a crucial period in her life—as a single mother. She is a semi-retired psychotherapist, living now in Santa Monica, Calif., with her poet/blogger husband, Norm Levine. Her poetry has appeared in numerous literary journals and was nominated for the 2012 Pushcart Prize.

Hubert Babinski, a retired academic and business man, is completing a memoir of his experiences in Poland from the early 1960s to the present. His story in this journal is an excerpt from that work.

Malea Baer is a writer and artist living in lower Westchester. She is an MFA candidate at Sarah Lawrence. She is also a single parent, homeschooling her 13-year-old son. Malea's writing has appeared in *The Sacramento Bee*, and her art has appeared on *LiteracyHead.com*.

John Black is an author who lives in Bronxville. His writing has been published in *Parnassus Literary Journal*, *The Comstock Review*, *Liguorian Magazine*, and other publications.

Juliana Broad is a writer aspiring to be a biologist. She took a gap year after high school, hiking and backpacking through Utah and Wyoming with an outdoor education program. She likes to think of herself as Edward Abbey. She is a freshman at McGill University

Donald Capone's stories have appeared in *Word Riot*, *Weekly Reader's READ*,

Thieves Jargon, and numerous anthologies His novel *Into the Sunset* was published in 2007. He lives in Hastings-on-Hudson.

Carla Carlson is a poet/writer in Pelham Manor. Her present themes emerge from a mindful review of her first twenty-five years with her husband and raising their five children in Westchester. She studies at the Writers Center at Sarah Lawrence and at the Hudson Valley Writers Center in Sleepy Hollow.

Rod Carlson was a helicopter pilot in Vietnam. He got an MBA at the University of Virginia and went on to a career in advertising and business consulting. He now lives in White Plains.

Michael Carman's most recent chapbook, *The Not,* was a finalist in the 2011 New Women's Voices contest, and will be published by Finishing Line Press this summer. Her first chapbook, *You in Translation,* was published by Toadlily Press. She teaches writing to art and design students at FIT/SUNY in Manhattan.

Jane Collins is the founder of the Poets at Pace reading series at Pace, where she teaches literature, film, and creative writing. Her poems and interviews have appeared in many journals. She lives with her son, Sam, in a small town on the Hudson River.

Clark Cooke has received rewards and fellowships from Hunter College; the University of California, Riverside; and the Purchase College Writer's Center. His work has been published by PANK Magazine and Connotation Press. He lists among his influences Dostoyevsky, John Edgar Wideman, Dave Chappelle, and the Marquis de Sade.

Bonnie Jill Emanuel is working on her first book of poetry, *Almost Ready.* She lives in Scarsdale with her husband and two sons. When she is not writing, she may be found cooking, kickboxing, or hiding out in bookstores.

Catherine Faurot holds an MFA from Bennington and an MALS degree from Dartmouth. Her poetry book, *Plow Harrow Seed,* was published in 2008, and her work has appeared in *Colorado Review, The New Orphic Review,* and *The Christian Century,* among other journals.

Campbell Geeslin lives in White Plains. He wrote a libretto based on one of his books for children, *How Nanita Learned to Make Flan.* The opera has had more than 200 performances. His book *Elena's Serenade* was named best read-aloud book for children in 2005.

Dylan Gilbert's stories have appeared in *Spilling Ink Review, Slow Trains, Sleet Magazine,* and *Word Riot,* among others, and he was recently nominated for the Pushcart Prize in fiction. He can be found online at *http://dylansstories.weebly.com/.*

Elizabeth L. Gould lives in Sleepy Hollow with her husband and twin sons. "The

Tintype" is linked to her novel *West of Center*, a story of love, betrayal, loss, and remaking one's life, set in East Texas in the early 1900s. Visit *www.elizabethlgould.com* for more information.

Holly Guran, author of *River Tracks* (Poets Corner Press), received an International Merit Award from *Atlanta Review*. Her poems have appeared in *Poetry East, Poet Lore,* and *Borderlands* and in the anthology *The Breath of Parted Lips* (Cavan Kerry Press). In 2012 she earned a Massachusetts Cultural Council award.

Madeline Hendricks has been writing plays for most of her adult life. She first gained recognition at age 17, winning the Fidelity FutureStage playwriting contest for *Driver's Education*. Since then, she has studied dramatic literature at George Washington University and received other awards, including the Luther Rice Fellowship.

Katherine Blaine Hurley is a graduate of the University of Pennsylvania and the Sarah Lawrence MFA program. She teaches writing at Purchase College SUNY. Katherine lives in New York, where she is currently at work on her first novel.

Mary Johnson was born in Bridgeport and grew up in western Connecticut. She graduated from Smith College, and now works as the teen librarian at the North Castle Public Library. "White-Tailed Deer" is based on an incident in her childhood. It is her first published poem.

Gillian Lynn Katz, born in South Africa, moved to the United States as a teenager. She won second place in the 41st Annual Greenburgh poetry competition. Her chapbook *Kaleidoscope* is forthcoming from Finishing Line Press. She has an MA in creative writing from Manhattanville. Her Web site is *http://gillianlynnkatz.net*

Brendan Kiernan lives in White Plains with his wife and son. "Sundowning" is his first published work.

Douglas Krohn is a physician in Briarcliff Manor. His fiction and essays have appeared in *The Westchester Review, The Einstein Quarterly Journal of Biology and Medicine,* and *The Scarsdale Inquirer*. He lives in Westchester with his wife and four sons.

Sheila Lamb is an MFA candidate in fiction at Queens University of Charlotte. Her work has appeared in *Monkeybicyle, Referential Magazine,* and elsewhere. Her story *Swim* was nominated for the Pushcart Prize. She has conducted extensive genealogy research in Westchester, where her ancestors worked in the marble quarries.

Sarah Levine received her BA in English from UMass Amherst and her MFA in poetry from Sarah Lawrence. Recent work has appeared in *Vinyl, decomP,* and *Metazen*. Levine has taught creative writing to seventh graders in Queens and to women at Valhalla Correctional Facility through The Right to Write program.

Michael Malone's writing has appeared in *The New York Times*, *San Francisco Chronicle*, *Westchester Magazine*, and *ESPN.com*. He runs the commuter blog *Trainjotting .com* and writes a weekly column for Captain Lawrence Brewing. He lives in Hawthorne with his wife, Susan; son, Gavin; daughter, Charlotte; kitten, Luna; and three unpublished novels.

Daphne Carter McKnight has taught and counseled college-age and adult students in New York for 30 years. She has published two chapbooks, *Full Grown and Female* and *Sister, Sing Me a Song*, and contributed work to *Art's Buoyant Felicity: An Anthology of Art/Creativity/Healing*; she has a poem posted on *www.VisionCarriers.com*.

Joan Motyka, an editor of *The Westchester Review*, was an editor at *The New York Times* for many years. Her journalistic work has appeared in *The New York Times*, *The Boston Globe*, *The International Herald Tribune*, and other publications. She also writes short stories and teaches memoir writing.

Loretta Oleck, a clinical psychotherapist and writer, received her MA in creative writing from NYU. Her poetry has been published in *Poetica Magazine*, *The Stone Hobo*, *Still Point Arts Quarterly*, and *Marco Polo Arts Magazine* and was read at The Hudson Valley Writer's Center's Readings on War and Peace.

Pamela Manché Pearce, a Garrison resident, was director of events and publicity for PEN American Center. Her work has been published here and abroad. She founded "Poets Read Poetry," a quartet of Hudson Valley poets who discuss poems on a theme at private meetings, on radio, and at public forums.

Jeffrey W. Peterson was a 2011 Fellow at the Bucknell Seminar for Younger Poets. He received his BA from the University of West Georgia and currently attends Sarah Lawrence, where he is pursuing an MFA in Poetry. His poems have appeared in *Eclectic* and *Prairie Margins*.

Sharon Medoff Picard lives and works in Westchester, where she is a psychoanalyst in private practice. *The Westchester Review* is her first effort at publication

Sue Prevost, born in New Orleans, had parents who "lived in story-telling mode." She and her siblings "swooned and dreamed [themselves] to sleep and grew up to travel the world." She has degrees in English and education. New to Westchester, she enjoys "discovering mountains, changing leaves, and black bears."

Richard Quigley is in his fourth year as a creative writing student at Purchase College, SUNY. His poetry has been featured in the campus-wide publications *The Submission*, *The Leaf Unturned*, and *Italics Mine*.

Pete Reilly trains at Aikido of Westchester in White Plains every morning and eats breakfast with an eclectic group of friends. He has published poetry in *Bluestem*, *Blotter*, *Perspectives*, *Blueline*, *Brink*, and other literary magazines; has written two novels; and is writing a work of nonfiction, "Teaching from the Inside-Out".

Allison Rosenthal is a sophomore at Sarah Lawrence, where she is studying languages, literatures, and history. Someday she hopes to work for a publishing company or a food magazine.

Maryann Stafford writes and tinkers with her ukulele in Yorktown Heights.

Sophia G. Starmack received an MA in French and Francophone literature from Bryn Mawr and is currently pursuing an MFA in poetry at Sarah Lawrence. She works as a teacher and tutor.

Meredith Trede's book *Field Theory* was published by SFA Press in 2011. A Toadlily Press founder, she published a chapbook, *Out of the Book*, in *Desire Path*. Her work has appeared in the journals *Barrow Street*, *Gargoyle*, and *The Paris Review*. She has won numerous fellowships, and a NYFA grant.

Susan V. Walton earned her MFA in poetry from Sarah Lawrence in 2003, but admits to a fierce addiction to language since childhood. Now a grandmother, she delights in adventures with her grandchildren, and has learned to love oysters. She is a psychotherapist in private practice in Westchester.

Jonathan Vatner, a staff writer at Hue, has written for *The New York Times* and O. With an MFA in fiction writing from Sarah Lawrence and a BA in cognitive neuroscience from Harvard, he has been published in *Best Gay Stories 2012* and the 2011 *Westchester Review*.

Fred Yannantuono, fired from Hallmark for writing meaningful greeting-card verse, finished 183rd at the 1985 U.S. Crossword Puzzle Tournament; won a yodeling contest in a German restaurant; was bitten by a guard dog in a tattoo parlor; survived a car crash with Sidney Lumet; hasn't been arrested in 17 months.

James K. Zimmerman won a Daniel Varoujan award and two Hart Crane Memorial poetry awards. His work appears or is forthcoming in *Anderbo.com*, *The Bellingham Review*, *Rosebud*, *Inkwell*, *Hawai'i Pacific Review*, and *Earth's Daughters*, among others. A former singer and songwriter, he is a clinical psychologist in private practice.

James H. Zorn grew up in Georgia. He taught English in Germany, the Philippines, Japan, and Spain and is a professor of English and creative writing at Bergen Community College, in New Jersey. He lives in Irvington with his wife and son. He is currently working on a novel.

Past Contributors

Lisa Argrette Ahmad

Floyd Albert

Seth Appel

Harley April

Ze'ev Aviezer

Debra Banerjee

Marlena Maduro Baraf

Donna Barkman

Alex Barnett

Jessica Bennett

Rosetta Benson

Kristina Bicher

Jonathan Billet

Sally Bliumis-Dunn

A. H. Block

Andrew Bomback

Mary Lou Butler-Buschi

Steve Cain

Carla Carlson

Rod Carlson

Daniel Carlyon

David Carlyon

Liane Kupferberg Carter

Linda Hillman Chayes

Llyn Clague

Stephanie Kaplan Cohen

Patrick Conley

Judy Coulter

Gillian Cummings

Ted Davis

P. J. DeGenaro

Mark Deitch

Lisa Fleck Dondiego

Arlene Edelson

Kevin Egan

Lee Eiferman

Sara Fasy

D. A. Feinfeld

Lya Ferreyra

Sheila Filipowski

Judith Naomi Fish

Katherine Flaherty

Jane Flanders

Lesleigh Forsyth

Patricia Anne Frame

Denise Mozilo Frasca

Nina Gabriele-Cuva

Eleanor Gaffney

Kate M. Gallagher

Campbell Geeslin

Diane Germano

Dylan Gilbert

Sophie Glass

Jacqueline Goldstein

Myrna Goodman

Joseph P. Griffith

Blythe Hamer

Ruth D. Handel

Jesse Hassenger

Lu Hauser

David Hellerstein

Werner Hengst

Adrienne Hernandez

Jack Hickey

Lauren Hilger

Catherine Hiller

Susan Hodara

Luann Jacobs

Kuniko Katz

Jean Katzenberg

Karen Kawaguchi

Autumn Kindelspire

Stephen Kling

Nathan Kolodney

Florence Reiss Kraut

Douglas Krohn

Joe Landau

Janice Landrum

Gloria Lazar

Sarah Levine

Linda Levitz

Steve Lewis

Lisa Romano Licht

Meg Lindsay

Pei-Ling Lue

Julia Mallach

Rich Manley

Eve Marx

Bill Maynard

Maura McCaw

Elizabeth Meaney

Merle Molofsky

Tania Moore

Joan Motyka

J. Mullee

John Thomas Murphy

Gunter Nitsch

Ruth Obernbreit

Loretta Oleck

Zachary Pace

Gary Percesepe

Don Peteroy

Sharon Medoff Picard

Kevin Pilkington

Mark Podwal

Holly Posner

Royal F. Potter

Ross Priel

Jeff Queen

Paul-John Ramos

Jocelyn Reznick

Robin Richardson

Shawn Rubenfeld

Alana Ruprecht

Thaddeus Rutkowski

Natalie Safir

Boria Sax

Sam Sax

Bill Scher

Steven Schnur

Cora Schwartz

Amy Ralston Seife

Emily Seife

Ruth Seldin

Galit and Gilad Seliktar

Neil Selinger

Ilene Semiatin

Roberta Silman

Rachel M. Simon

Linda Simone

Jena Smith

Stanley Sokol

Gloria Donen Sosin

A. L. Steindorff

Todd Strasser

Barry Roark Strutt

Laurie Sullivan

Angela Derecas Taylor

Allen M. Terdiman

Meredith Trede

Sergio Troncoso

Joanna Valente

Jonathan Vatner

Les Von Losberg

Elisabeth von Uhl

Betty Wald

Catherine Wald

Dale Walkonen

Charlotte Walsh

Jeff Wanshel

James L. Weil

Barbara Weinreb

Missy Egan Wey

Kate Wheeler

Kathleen Williamson

Tracy P. Williamson

Hilton Wilson

Rachel Wineberg

Elaine K. Winik

Amelia B. Winkler

Mark Wisniewski

Catherine Wolf

Celestine Woo

Elizabeth Wood

Peter Wood

Fred Yannantuono

Joyce Zaritsky

Judy Zendell

James K. Zimmerman

SUPPORTERS

We gratefully acknowledge
a generous grant from a
Westchester family foundation.

Louis Albert
Mary and Steve Borowka
William H. Forsyth, Jr.
Sandy and George Gottlieb
RoseAnn and George Hermann
Ann and Paul Spindel
Sheila and Burton Stone
Jonathan P. Terdiman
Madhulika G. Varma

Anonymous

BOOKSELLERS
Anderson's Book Shop
    Larchmont, N.Y.
Arcade Booksellers
    Rye, N.Y.
Galápagos Books
    Hastings-on-Hudson, N.Y.
The Village Book Shop
    Pleasantville, N.Y.
Womrath Book Shop
    Bronxville, N.Y.

OTHER MERCHANTS
Amazon.com
Designer One
    Larchmont, N.Y.
Futterman's Stationery
    Larchmont, N.Y.
Silver Tips Tea Room
    Tarrytown, N.Y.